Kitchen Makeover on a Budget

A Step-by-Step Guide to Getting a Whole New Kitchen for Less

By: Larry Jacobs

ISBN-13 **978-1494277727**

TABLE OF CONTENTS

Larry Jacobs

*To my dad, who taught me how to do
most of the things in this book such as budgeting,
planning, remodeling, designing, plumbing,
tiling, electrical wiring, painting,
how to save money on projects,
and how to work with contractors
and much more.*

INTRODUCTION

There are many different kitchen cabinet brands out in the market place. Most are very expensive if they have any quality to them. Most of the low priced cabinets are cheaply made with virtually no premium features.

Most people today want high quality premium cabinets. That is one of the reasons that people want a new kitchen. There is only one exception to this that I have found and that is the IKEA kitchens. The IKEA kitchen offers you attractive affordable cabinets with all of the premiums features of expensive cabinets.

IKEA gives you a very nice European styled kitchen on a low budget. These units are impressively engineered prefabricated cabinets. If you are willing to do some work and understand and learn basic kitchen remodeling you can save quite a bit of money. I am talking about saving thousands of dollars with today's kitchen prices.

As an owner of a new IKEA kitchen, I have learned from the ground up all the basics of how to plan and put together a complete kitchen on a budget.

In this book you will learn how to completely design and put together a fantastic kitchen. You can do it all yourself or hire a contractor to do it for you. Since you know how it should be done by this book you can then watch a contractor and know if he is building it correctly. You'll know exactly what it will cost you. The cost of your cabinets won't be the financial road block that kills your kitchen project. You'll know from this book everything you need to do from beginning to end to get your new kitchen. You'll know how to spend your money in the right places and at the right time.

First thing I need to tell you about the IKEA cabinets are when to buy them. IKEA has a 20% off sales special about four times during the year. These sales events include the cabinets, appliances and accessories.

What you want to do is to first read this book, design your new kitchen using IKEA's kitchen planner and my instructions. Then just wait for those 20% off sales specials and jump on it immediately to order your kitchen.

When their sales start, they generally have all the kitchen parts, but if you wait to the end of the sale, they may be out of some of the items. To insure you get your entire kitchen components, be ready with your order and put it in as soon as the sale starts.

OK, now let's start. The first thing you want to know is how much is your IKEA kitchen going to cost? It depends on several factors:

1) The size of your kitchen.
2) The cost of the IKEA kitchen materials and appliances you choose.
3) The cost of labor in your area and how much of the work you are going to do yourself.

First, you might do this as I did. Go out and get some estimates from various big box stores such as Lowes, Home Depot and some local kitchen redesign stores. You'll need measurements of your kitchen room such as length, width, and height of the room. Take several pictures of the kitchen and know if you want to make any changes such as tearing out a wall, moving electrical, tearing out soffits, etc. Ask their kitchen designers to do a basic design for you and give you an estimate. From this you will actually get some good early design ideas.

I personally took my sketch with measurements of the room and a rough estimate of what I wanted in cabinet design, plus several pictures of my current kitchen to Home Depot, Lowes, KitchenLand and CliqStudios. They all gave me similar layouts. That helped me of what the kitchen design should look like. Prices ranged from a low of $10,000 up to $20,000. The average was $15,000. Let me say also, that none of the estimates included installation or any premium features. If I wanted the premium features it would cost another 50% for labor and add another 50% for premium features. So for just a small 10' x 10' kitchen, the cost for new cabinets' average was $15,000. So the additional labor would add another $7,500 and for premium features that would add another $7,500. So the cost of my kitchen remodeling with premium features and installed would be $30,000! Now if you add granite counter tops on to that the price would be around $35,000!

For a premium kitchen at IKEA that I now have, I paid just $4,000 for the cabinets and $3,500 for the granite counter tops. I did buy the cabinets during the IKEA 20% off sale and the granite counter tops during one of Home Depot's counter top sale.

The cabinets are just as nice as the $30,000 cabinets from other stores and they even have a 25 year guarantee! The countertop is premium granite with a 15 year guarantee. So it cost me around $7,500 instead of $35,000.

For most premium kitchen cabinets at IKEA it generally costs around $3,000 - $8,000. Appliances are extra and labor is not included.

This book is a step-by-step program of how to remake your old kitchen into a new IKEA premium kitchen on a budget. I will also tell you how to get help, like hiring a contractor or how to hire professionals to do jobs you can't do such as electrical, plumbing or dry walling.

If you are planning to remodel you're your old kitchen into a new IKEA beautiful kitchen. This is the book to read. From a person who really did it.

I am not a kitchen designer, but I understand the whole process better than they do, as I got my hands dirty from tearing out the cabinets, wall, electrical to installing new lights, plumbing and new cabinets. There is a lot more to this than just designing it on paper as a designer does. I did take some engineering classes in college and have a master's degree in business.

I have created this book so that you will have all the knowledge and how-to-do-it explanations and tips so that you can get the best kitchen for your money. Even if you already have the best idea of what you want to do, this book will help you in making the right important decisions and possibly avoid many of the common kitchen pitfalls that many make in remodeling their kitchen.

For some time my wife and I discussed that our 30-year old kitchen needed a facelift. We had the traditional oak cabinets with the yellowing finish that you have seen in many homes built in the 70s. We discussed repainting them with a color. What color should it be? Should we spray the paint on or brush it on. Or maybe getting a cabinet refinishing kit from RUST-OLEUM that is available everywhere. Or should we reface all the doors with new doors that feature hinges that are hidden. What about hardware like knobs and hinges? Should those be changed?

We would also need to replace the countertop. Should we get Formica, granite, and some other stone countertop? But one hates to put expensive granite on old cabinets, even if they are refinished. That is probably just a waste of money.

What is wrong with using the old cabinets? The main problem is that the carpenters that put them in 30 years ago did not have any of the new hardware features that makes today's premium cabinets so nice. I am talking about lazy susans hardware in the corner cabinets, the large pull out doors, pantries and much more. The old cabinets did not have that finish look such as enclosing the refrigerators with side panels or finishing the tops and bottoms of the cabinets with fancy moldings. Also most of the old cabinets are built under soffits that make the cabinets short and did not have the look or space of today's beautiful tall cabinets.

Another factor that I had heard about is that an IKEA kitchen can substantially increase of value of your house. For example, recently I heard that there were a couple of houses with new IKEA kitchens in them in Kansas City. They were put up for sale and there were bidding wars on these houses largely because of the IKEA kitchens. The IKEA kitchen raised the price of these houses by $20,000 - $30,000!

Sure you can paint your old cabinets, or replace the doors, but that is not going to upgrade your kitchen like a brand new IKEA cabinets and it's not going to raise the price of your house by $20,000 - $30,000.

You should figure out how much it is going to cost you to put in an IKEA kitchen. Then if you can justify it then you need to do it. It is an excellent investment in both your living style and the return in money if you should sell your house. Also in the back of the book I recommend cooking software that will enable you to plan meals every day of the week in your new kitchen and improve your health and start eating better food and end eating out at fast food restaurants. In this book I will give you the ideas that will save you a ton of money.

Before I started this project I had been to IKEA several times and had remembered how nice their cabinets were that were displayed in their show rooms. So I checked out on the internet about what many IKEA customers were saying.

Almost all the ratings were very positive.

I understood that one can actually design your own kitchen using their online 3D Kitchen planner. So I went online and designed our kitchen with their software. I did get a lot of my ideas from the kitchen designers that I contacted earlier. That made it very easy to design my kitchen. It did help also that I did have some engineering classes in college.

It took about 3-hours to do it, but I knew what I wanted from the kitchen designers I talked to earlier. Most of the time, I was just learning to use the software. The first design I put together was not exactly what I really wanted so I came back to the site every day for the next week and played with the design and tweaked it until it looked perfect. My design was better than what the kitchen designers gave me.

When I was totally satisfied with the design I pushed the IKEA button that lists the parts and price of the kitchen. It totaled up to around $4,500.

I waited until the next IKEA 20% off kitchen sale and then jumped on it. It dropped the price to around $3,900 and that would be a dramatic saving over the $10,000 - $30,000 prices of the other kitchen designed that I had received from IKEA's competitors.

So when you are ready to jump on it with the IKEA sale, you first make sure the kitchen design is ready. Then you call IKEA and tell them you have the kitchen you want to buy totally designed online and saved. Give them your username and password. They will pull it up and go through it to make sure everything is correct. They may ask you several questions and make some changes. Then they will produce the list of items with a total price. They will also check inventory to make sure it is all there in their warehouse. If it is they will tell you that you have 24 hrs to come in and purchase and pick up your kitchen.

By the way if you live near an IKEA, it is better to just come in and do this with one of their kitchen experts.

I had to do mine by phone since I lived 6 hours away. I also explained this to them that I lived some distance away and I would have to rent a truck when I got there and drive back. The IKEA warehouse was in Frecso, TX and I was in Springfield, Missouri.

So we drove to Fresco in our car, and in Fresco we rented a U-Haul truck with a car tow attachment. Paid for and picked up the kitchen and drove back the next day. IKEA completely loaded the entire kitchen in the U-Haul. They will do it if you ask them.

The next day, we unloaded the kitchen into our garage and took the U-Haul truck back to the local U-Haul site in Springfield. By the way, before you rent a U-Haul truck check local truck rental companies. U-Haul will match their prices. This will save you usually 20 – 30%.

The next step was to remove the old cabinets from the kitchen.

So in this book, I'll explain to you how to remove your old kitchen and how to install a new IKEA kitchen. Yes, I am going to teach everything you need to know. I want you to be in the driver's seat of this project. You can do it yourself or hire a contractor to do it. I'll tell you how to do that also, without losing control.

So yes, there are two ways to do it. One way is to do it yourself. The other way is to hire a contractor. You can also hire some workers to do part or even all of your work. If you choose to hire a contractor you need to know how to handle him and I'll explain it later in this book so you can get your money's worth.

Are you ready to get started in building your new IKEA beautiful kitchen? Are you excited?

PLANNING

How Long Will it Take?

There are factors that play into an IKEA kitchen renovation project, but the construction part of the renovation is from four weeks to possible up to 6 months. If you plan it right and have all the materials on site and you are not going to tear out soffits, move plumbing, electric or gas you could possibly have it done in 4 weeks. Every project is different as every kitchen size and shape is different. There are also possible surprises that you might have so you should plan for that and have a contingency plan for such just in case. Every kitchen project has problems, so work with them when they come. Any problem can be taken care of with some time and the right knowledge. Just take the problems as a challenge.

What about a Contractor?

If you are hiring a contractor you have the possibility of many things going wrong. It is not like doing it yourself. You, of course, have total control over yourself, but you don't have total control over a contractor.

You might just get lucky and get a really good contractor. But on the other hand you might get a bad contractor that will give you problems, delays and might even quit and leave the project. There are many strategies that you can use to avoid the many problems you can get with a contractor.

A contractor has many customers and you don't want to be the last one on his schedule so make sure you have all the materials on your site and are ready for the project for the contractor and his workers. If the contractor has to wait for something he probably will move on to another project and may or may not come back later.

Don't pay the contractor until the kitchen project is completely done. Paying him early could be a big mistake. You could pay him partially in the beginning and pay the remaining balance when the job is completely done. You need to set up a payment schedule that you can both agree to.

Make a completion date in writing with the contractor so there is no excuse to let it drag on. There should even be penalties for not completing on time.

Are you planning on hiring out a lot of work?

If you are planning to hire out a lot of the work it is recommended to get a general contractor for the project and this is why.

Scheduling is very complex and challenging it could drive you nuts. It is difficult to get all the various trades such as plumbing, electric, dry walling to coordinate all of their schedules and be there at the right times. For example, the plumbing and electric needs to be done before the walls are put up and closed. Because of this there will be a lot of emails and phone calls are done to coordinate this. Contractors have established relationships with the trade people and they can get them to show up when there are supposed to.

The contractor is knowledgeable and can check on the progress of the work. He knows what to look for. You probably don't know what to look for. Is the work being done properly? A very good contractor should follow everything being done and make sure it is done right.

The contractor has time dedicated to the project and can come by and continually check the progress and can oversee the work. Do you have the time to do this? Most people don't have this time if you work at another job, which you probably do.

To find a good contractor you might check out Angie's List. You can also ask friends of who they recommend. You should get three different bids from contractors. The bidding progress will give you an idea as to what the price should be. If the bids are all around the same price then you'll know you're on the right track of what you should pay. The clue to this is how responsive is the contractor to your questions, emails, and phone calls. If he does not get back to you right away then probably you should drop him as a contractor prospect, because this is what will happen when the job starts. Also ask for references from previous clients from the contractor. If he can't give you any references then drop him.

Ask previous clients about the details of the work that was done, the schedule that was followed and how they paid him. Ask did he return phone calls? Did he stay on the schedule and finish on time? Did he stay on budget? Where there any problems? Did the subcontractors do their jobs correctly and on time? Did he coordinate the project so you did not have to get involved?

You should look for a contractor right away if you are not planning of doing most of the work yourself. Have him come by and look at the basic floor plan and discuss the project and ask for his input and that give you some helpful ideas. Even if you decide not to use the contractor, his ideas will still help you a lot.

You need the contractor to give you a firm bid on the project and make sure he understands the entire project and all the materials chosen. There are many contractors you can contact for free estimates. Get them into your kitchen and ask them exactly what they can do and the estimated cost.

Many of them won't want to be pinned down in an exact cost. They mainly want to get their feet in your door and then charge additional ongoing charges.

If you plan to use contractors for all the work done, then for a small to medium kitchen prepare to pay $4,000 - $8,000 in labor.

If you plan to do most of the work then you will still need to have the electrical and plumbing needs to be done by professionals. Sometimes their work must meet city codes and you won't be able to do this work.

Permits

You should call the local city permit office and get the costs for your necessary permits to remodel a kitchen. The permits for a normal size kitchen can cost from $300 to $1,000. If you are moving or changing windows or some outside walls you might even need more permits.

Check List for Estimates of the Various Costs

1) Design Service
2) City Permits
3) Removing Your Old Cabinets
4) Removing Your Old Flooring
5) Preparing Floor Surface & Installing New Floor
6) Removing Trash
5) Removing Old Walls
6) New Drywall
7) Plumbing
8) Electrical
9) Assembling cabinets
10) Installing cabinets
11) Installing appliances
12) Installing lights
13) Cleaning up afterwards

Sample Labor Costs

1) Removing the old cabinets	$600 - $1000
2) Electrical	$500 - $2000
3) Drywall	$500 - $1000
4) Floor removal	$500 - $2000
5) Cabinet installation	$2000 - $4000
6) Countertop	$500 - $5000
7) Appliance installation	$500 - $800
8) Plumbing	$500 - $1500
9) Lighting installation	$500 - $1000
10) Flooring installation	$1000 - $5000

List of Needed Supplies

Now is the time for you to put the list together and order the supplies. You need everything on your list such as IKEA cabinets, lumber, plywood, braces, light cans, LED lights, electrical wire, electrical switches, sockets, connectors, flooring.

Also don't forget to order drywall and patching plaster. Order and have delivered even wall, ceiling and trim paint, brushes, rollers.

Deliveries should be scheduled according to the construction schedule.

You should check on lead times as some things take longer to arrive than others.

Make sure everything is in stock and not back ordered. Having any missing items may delay your entire project.

Plan to Eat Out a Lot

You should plan to eat out a lot during this project. You can use your bathroom sink to wash some dishes. You can have your refrigerator, microwave and coffee pot in a different location. You can also use paper plates, glasses and plastic spoons, knives, forks and paper napkins.

Use prepared foods (or anything you can cook in a microware) and that can save of lot of the expense of eating out.

Prepare and Protect Against Dust

Make sure to protect against possible dust. You should have dust control for this project. That means sealing out the kitchen from the rest of the house with plastic sheeting between the rooms. This plastic can even have something called a zip wall zipper in the plastic. The demolition is very messy! Expect a lot of dust.

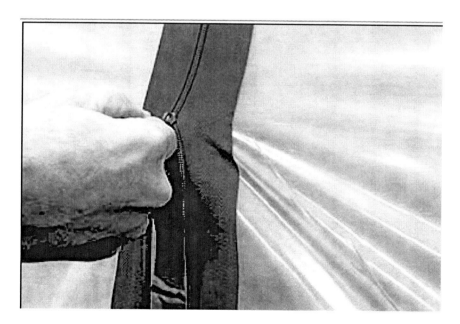

Miracle Sears Sander

This Sears vibrating sander really helps a lot with dust. I tried several brands but nothing works like this one. Connected to a Shop-Vac it eliminates almost all the dust. It is quite a miracle sander. It is expensive, around $100, but just go ahead and buy it if you are going to do any drywall sanding!

A Shop-Vac with long hose is necessary and should be used in combination with the Sear's vibrating sander.

Three parts to your kitchen remodeling project:

1. The first part is to prepare the kitchen by removing the old cabinets, soffits, floor and rearranging electrical, plumbing and walls.
2. The second is designing your kitchen by using IKEA kitchen 3D software.
3. The third part is installing your IKEA kitchen.

PREPARE THE KITCHEN

1. Remove most of the appliances. Keep some appliances you might need such as the refrigerator, the sink and faucet. If you are going to sell some appliances you might post them on Craigslist. We kept our refrigerator, stove and dishwasher since they were all purchased within the last 2-years.

2. Empty all of the cabinets from the area in put the items in a safe area, dust free. Probably in extra unused bedroom would work fine. Don't stack the items next to the kitchen otherwise you'll speed many hours getting the dust off.

3. Get a perimeter area outside of the kitchen for tools and the materials. You'll need this space to work in.

4. Put up temporary plastic walls to protect the rest of the house from dust. Use zipper doors. Cover any furniture with plastic. This will save you from cleaning up later on.

5. Make a house key for the contractor if you use one and setup work times with restrictions and delivery times.

6. If you hire a contractor, you need to have him come in explain everything from start to finish. Put together an agreement together with a penalty if it is not finished on time. Understand that there can be no changes to the agreement once it is made.

7. Warranty is a good idea to cover the work that contractor or his subcontractors do.

8. Setup a payment schedule. Best to give 1/3 up front for labor and materials to get the job rolling. Pay the rest based on milestones completed and hold up the final payment until the job is completely finished. There should be an itemized detail list of everything to be done such as cabinetry, hardware, fixtures, tile, etc. Make sure brands are listed. This should all be clear in the work contract. If you are letting the contractor buy the items check prices online so that he is not overcharging. If you are buying the items buy from just a few suppliers, be

available for deliveries and finally check for damage or for any missing pieces.

9. Stay in touch with the contractor during the project and know the best times to contact him or for him to contact you. There will be many questions he may need to ask you so you should be available. During work times keep out of the way with workers so nothing is delayed. Put together a paper trail on the contact and what was said. Keep a close eye on the work and ask questions if necessary.

10. After the work is all done check for anything such as dings in walls or anything damaged by workers

Trash

You need to get either a dumpster or plan to take out a lot every week in your regular trash container. If you do the remodeling yourself then using your own trash container will work. Ask your trash company to give you another trash can. Most of them will do it with no charge. If you hire a contractor who uses many workers you must get at least a small dumpster that will cost around $300.

I personally just used the weekly trash removal to get rid the old kitchen. It took several weeks, but I saved $300.

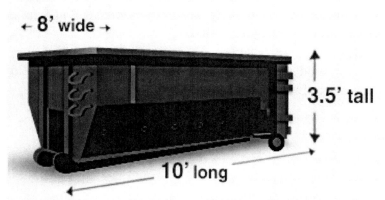

Removing the Old Cabinets

Here is a picture of our old kitchen. Look at the old oak cabinets, soffits and old ceiling light. Look familiar to your kitchen?

Do a good job in removing the cabinets and try not to damage them. If they are in excellent shape you can donate them to the Habitat for Humanity. You can possibly take part of the donation off your income taxes. Just call Habitat for Humanity and ask for a pickup. It saves you a lot a work and time of disposing of the old cabinets and the donation helps low income people. We donated our cabinets to them.

If you have a garage or a basement and want a workshop the old cabinets can best used for that purpose.

Removing Soffits

Removing soffits is very difficult. They usually are built in and nailed into the ceiling supports. In the next picture you see the soffits and then one of the following picture what it looked like after they were removed.

You'll need a crowbar, a pry bar and a sledge hammer plus a ladder to get this done, if you are doing the work.

Get the Little Giant Aluminum Ladder

Consider getting the 6' little giant aluminum ladder. It is light weight and you'll need it a lot for this kitchen project. A ladder like this will be used over and over again on this kitchen project. You will use it for removing the old cabinets, removing the soffits, rewiring the kitchen, dry walling, removing and adding new walls, removing popcorn ceilings, painting and putting up the new wall cabinets and molding.

You can't do it without this ladder1

More Work After the Soffits are Gone

Now in this picture you see the soffits are gone. It leaves a big hole in the ceiling which means a lot of work. If you notice the drain exhaust pipe and electrical wires need to be removed and new drywall needs to be put back up. Ceiling popcorn needs to be scraped and the light needs to come down and be replaced.

Removing Old Lights

Removing old lights is difficult. Please make sure the power is shut off. You might also use ropes to make it a safe take down. You don't want the light falling on you.

With the rope attached gently pry the light box off the wall and give the rope slack and let it come down slowly so it won't hit and injure you.

Protect Yourself with a Voltage Tester

The electrical wires in the soffits need to be rerouted and disconnected. When working with electricity always use a voltage tester to make sure the power is off. Don't touch any hot wire and assume that it is dead. Always check it to see if it is hot. Use the Fluke Volt-Alert AC Non-Contact tester pictured here. You can buy one of these at Home Depot or Lowes.

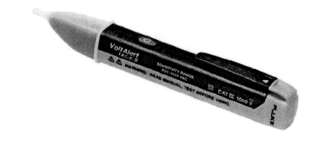

Rearranging Electrical

The electrical can be a big problem. I had an estimate to rearrange the wires in our soffits. The cost was $2,100. I have done electrical wiring before, so I took on the project myself. It took several days to complete the task. If you take on this project you need electrical wire, wire cutter, wire connectors, drill bits and wire strapping. You will need to rearrange the wires so they don't interfere with your drywall. Sometimes wire can be threaded through the 2x4s using a wood bit to make the holes. Sometimes it is easier to drill at the edge of the 2x4 and use a metal strap. You will need to do both to reroute the electrical. You'll need the following tools and supplies to get the electrical job done.

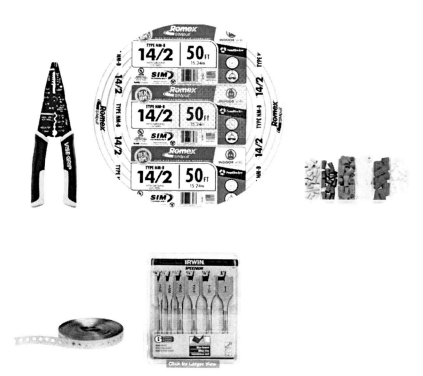

If you are going to keep basically the same layout of your kitchen at this time you need to check to make sure there are enough electrical outlets on your kitchen counters so you can use such things as mixers, blenders, toasters, electric knives, etc. Check for your local codes as this applies to your outlets. Some codes specify that you have an outlet every 3 feet in the kitchen.

Your appliances also need outlets and some require 220 lines. Make sure you know exactly where the outlets need to be as they are difficult to move once they are installed. Now is the time to install the new wiring or to have an electrician do it. In most cases let an electrician do this.

If you plan to have an electrician do the rearranging the wiring as well as putting in new sockets, switches and recessed lighting and connection to the garbage disposal then prepare to pay $600 to $2000 for this service.

Every modern kitchen needs recessed lighting. Putting them in usually takes electrical cans. Use a circle hole saw to save time drilling the holes in the ceiling. Also you need a lithium cordless drill. You'll use it in many different parts of this project.

Get LED lights that will last 30 years. Install dimmer switches as the LED lights will be too bright. The recessed lighting should be spaced at 3 feet apart and right above the edge of the cabinets. If you are planning on using under cabinet lighting you might install an electrical socket that can be turned on from one of the light switches on the wall. Most LED under the cabinet lighting connects to sockets with a transformer plug.

Putting in electrical cans is time consuming

You'll need to first cut the holes in the ceiling with the hole saw. Then string the wires from one can to the next using electrical connectors. It is time consuming. It took me a day to install nine lights in my kitchen.

Here is the illustration of my kitchen and the 9 lights placed directly above the edge of the cabinets and over the sink area. The lights again should be 3 feet apart.

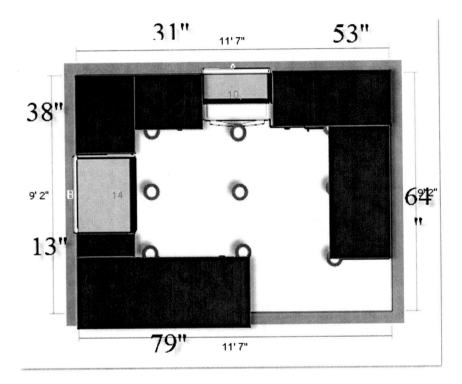

The tools you need for this part of the project are the hole saw, the drill, the electrical cans, electrical wire and connectors. This part of the project may take a couple of days depending on the number of lights you are installing.

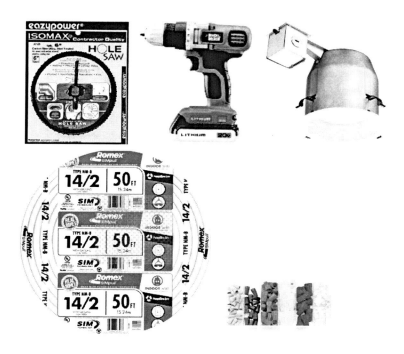

Types of Lighting

What types of lighting are available for your kitchen? There are three:

1. Ceiling lighting such as recessed or surface mounted

2. Under-cabinet lighting

3. Pendant lighting – the type that is generally over an island

The most popular is a combination of the above such as recessed lighting, under-cabinet lighting and pendants over the island.

Based on the needs of my kitchen, I felt that we only need recessed ceiling lights and under-cabinet lighting.

LED lighting is now popular and is replacing halogen in under counter lighting. Why use LED lighting? Because it is much more energy efficient and does not give off the heat that halogen does. Also it is very easy to install.

You May Want to Use an Electrician for Recessed Lighting

In many towns and cities building codes require the replacement of incandescent light in the kitchens and these must pass inspection. This will have to be done by licensed electrician. The inspectors will insure the electrician did the work correctly. If it is not done according to code it must be removed and done again correctly. Most new kitchens now are getting LED recessed lighting. These are in can lights which costs around $20.00 each. LEDs are $30 - $40 each. Installation of each can cost up to $75 each. .

Removing Drain Vents Pipes

Many soffits contain electrical wires and some contain vent pipes as ours did. Just use a hacksaw to remove any drain vent pipes in the soffits. You don't need this vent pipe anymore. The vent pipe can now be replaced with a sure-vent air admittance valve.

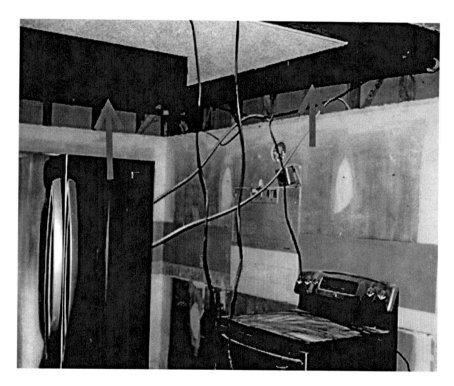

After removing the vent pipe you will have to install a sure-vent air admittance valve under your sink when you setup your cabinets and connect plumbing. This valve replaces the vent pipes and allows the drain to work properly. It is no longer necessary to vent the drain up through the roof. Air admittance valves are standard for islands in kitchens where it is an impossibility to vent through the roof.

Removing Old Flooring

Removing old flooring can be easy or difficult. Nailed down wood can easily come off, but if you have linoleum, engineered wood or tile that is glued down it is necessary to scrape off the old glue which can be time consuming. This can be very labor intensive and extremely costly. Some charge $2.50 per square foot to remove the old flooring and $2 per square foot to install new flooring. If you are doing it you'll need to use the pry bar, sledge hammer, knee pads and work gloves.

Replacing Subflooring

If your kitchen has particle board as part of the subfloor, you might need to replace it with plywood. Builders used particle board a lot in the 70s in houses. Later it was found that it was a poor subfloor. It quickly deteriorates when it gets wet. This was the case of our kitchen. We removed the particle board and replaced it with plywood with the same exact thickness.

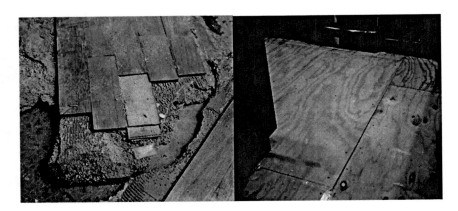

Gas Lines

Gas lines are extremely dangerous. A hard pipe comes out of the wall and if it is not in the right location it won't fit the range. It is very wise to download the PDF giving you installation instructions of the range. A licensed plumber needs to do this correctly and put it in the right location. Don't mess with it. Let a professional do it.

Removing Popcorn Ceiling

Removing the popcorn ceiling is easy to do. Just spray the ceiling with water using a sprayer of some type. Let it set for 15 minutes. Then scrape the popcorn off the ceiling using a drywall taping knife. Then spay it again, let stand for another 15 minutes and scrape off any popcorn left.

Here is a look at our ceiling with the popcorn. It was easy to remove and looked much better when it was gone.

Drywall

Drywall is a critical part of your kitchen project. It is recommended to hire a skilled person in this area. It takes years of experience to be able to do a good job in dry walling. It is an art in itself.

Repairing and or changing walls can be very difficult. Sometimes it is necessary to completely remove all the old sheet rock or plaster walls and replace it with needed sheet rock. Sometimes the entire room needs to be done. Sheet rock is very difficult to work with. If you want a good job hire a professional for this. For a 10' x 10' kitchen expect to pay $600 - $800.

If you want to attempt to work with drywall, you'll need the right tools listed below. The installation is to first cut the drywall panels to fit the wall. Use the utility knife and square for accurate cuts. Cut on one side, bend it over and then cut the other side of the panels. Attach the panels to the wall using drywall screws. Cut all of the openings in the wall for sockets using a jab saw. Next tape all the seams and cover the seams with the drywall compound. Let it dry for 24 hrs. Next sand the surface with heavy grit sandpaper. Then do another cover of the seams with the drywall compound, let dry for 24 hours and sand again with medium grit sandpaper. Finally do the last cover with the drywall compound and then let it dry for another 24 hours and sand with finishing sandpaper.

Sanding and dust control is very important. Use the Craftsman Sander with the Shop-Vac Dust Collection was the best way to go. This is a miracle tool. Almost all the dust was sucked up using a Shop-Vac connected to this excellent sander. You'll need drywall screws, drill, drywall panels, a knife, jab saw, scoring square, taping knife, mud pan, tape, joint compound, dust free sander, Shop-Vac, dust mask and goggles.

Drywall Tools

Drywall Dust Elimination Tools

Removing Walls

Today having the open concept is popular. You might need to remove a wall as I did in this kitchen. Always check with an engineer to see if the wall is load bearing and if it can be removed. This was a wall between the kitchen and the dining room which I removed. It took a day to remove it. Also notice it has one electric socket that had to be eliminated and a switch for the garbage disposal that had to be moved to another wall.

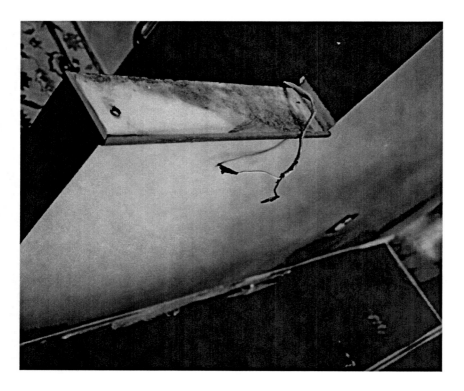

Extending a Wall

Extending a wall can be time consuming. It is easy to do. Just build a frame with 16-inch centers using 2x4s. I used construction screws instead of nails as they are much stronger. Also you may need to put in an electrical socket as I did in this case. Always use the level to make sure it is straight.

This is what the kitchen looked like after I put up the new dry wall and the new recessed lighting. It looked very nice, but took a lot of work.

IKEA KITCHEN COMPONENTS

If your room ready for the cabinets it is time for the next step.

Next go on the IKEA site and design your kitchen if you have not already done so using the 3D modeling software. How to use the software is included in the next section of this book.

Prepare to design the kitchen and place the order for everything selected from IKEA and pick it up or have it delivered.

Some Quick Ideas of How to Lower Your Costs

There are ways to save on the IKEA cabinets. I have listed them below:

1. First wait to buy the IKEA kitchen cabinets during their 4 quarterly sales of 20% off.
2. Choose a lower cost IKEA door style.
3. Buy appliances on sale at IKEA during the same sale.
4. Assemble the IKEA frames and knobs, handles by yourself.
5. Put new flooring where exposed and not under the cabinets.

B. Designing Your Kitchen

In designed your IKEA kitchen, these are the parts you need to be concerned with:

Cabinets Parts
Cabinets
Knobs
Sink
Faucet
Countertop

Appliances
Stove
Refrigerator
Vent hood
Trash Compactor
Microwave

Base Cabinets

Cabinets are made up of two separate parts. One part is the box and the other part is the door. The box is generally made up of particle board. The density and finish of this board is important. IKEA uses high density particle material in their base cabinets making them stronger than most of their competitors. The box comes in two separate finishes. One is a birch look and the other is white. The finish is melamine. You need to choose what works best with the door style you have chosen. The following pictures show some of the IKEA boxes. I chose the birch look. Here is a look at their base cabinets with shelves.

This is the corner wall cabinet with the lazy susan build in.

Here is a base corner cabinet with pull out shelves.

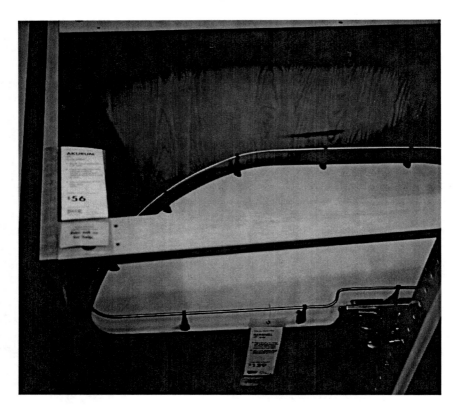

Doors and Drawers

Doors come in many different styles. IKEA has the best idea in using what is called full overlay doors. That means the doors cover the entire front of the box. They have hinges that enable them to open without hitting the other doors. The hinges are also hidden when the doors are closed. The hinges are very high quality.

Drawers are very important and carry generally the same style as the doors. These are premium doors. They are full extension doors so you can actually access everything even in the back of the drawers. Yes, the drawers can be pulled all the way out. This is a very nice feature not available in most other kitchen cabinets. These doors also come with a soft close hardware feature, which is nice.

Knobs and Handles

IKEA carries a good assortment of high quality knobs and handles at the right price. It is nice to be able to take them over and match the colors with the front doors and countertops.

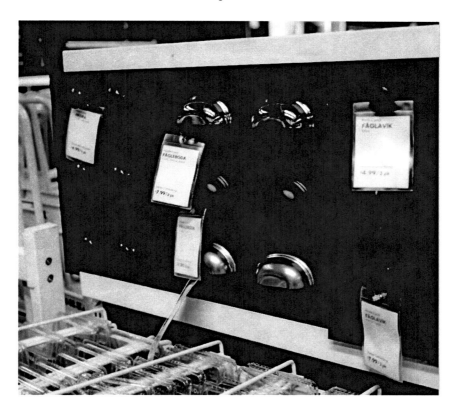

Matching Knobs with Doors and Countertops

As I said earlier it is very important to physically match knobs directly with the doors and countertop you will be using. IKEA makes this easy to do in their showrooms.

You can also match the counter tops with the cabinets and knobs. In my case I wanted black granite so even though I did not use IKEA's it was still nice to be able to match them and see what it looks like with a black IKEA countertop.

Toe kick

The toe kick is the recessed piece at the bottom of the cabinet. It gives you space for your feet. With IKEA cabinets most usually use the same color and finish on the toe kick as the doors and drawers have.

IKEA has a large assortment of toe kick colors exactly matching the door's colors that are available.

Crown Molding

Moldings give a great look to the cabinets. They are in the same finish as the doors and drawers. They go on both the tops and bottoms of the cabinets. The top moldings are called crown and are generally used for style. The moldings on the bottoms of the cabinets are used to hide cabinet lighting.

Cabinet Styles & Cost

If you go to an IKEA store or go online, you will find out that IKEA has over 20 various styles of cabinets. These styles have different funny names such as LIXTORP or SOFTIELUND. These are the styles for the cabinet fronts, doors, cover panels, trims, crown molding and toe kicks, etc.

IKEA uses the same frames for all of their cabinets. No matter what style of cabinet you pick, you will still use the same frames.

The cost of your cabinets will vary with:

The number of cabinets you pick.
The door style you select.
The various types of cabinets you pick.

To price your cabinets you need to design your kitchen using the IKEA website software. After the kitchen is designed the software will generate a complete parts list. This will give you the actual cost of the cabinets and parts needed.

In this book there is a section that explains exactly how to use the IKEA design software.

Cabinet Panels

Cabinet panels are used beside the refrigerator, dishwashers, and on islands. They come in different sizes, the largest being the 3' x 8'. They don't show up in the configurator so you'll have to manually order them when needed.

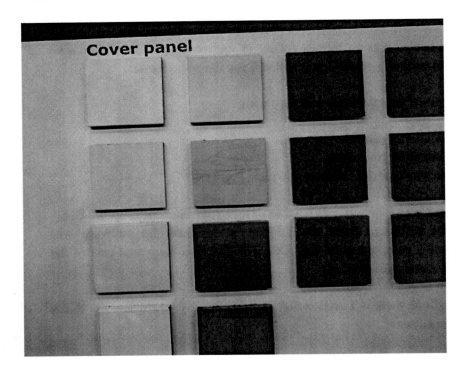

Cabinet Legs

The cabinet legs come in two types' plastic and stainless steel. Using these you can easily level the cabinets on floors. Most just order the black which are inexpensive, since they are covered with the toe kicks. The stainless steel is used when you want the legs to show.

Counter Tops

Your counter top is extremely important as to how your kitchen will look. Prices vary based on the type of material used. Some laminates cost $5 per square foot. Butcher blocks run around $5 per square foot. Granite can cost from $39 to $100 per square foot. You should shop around to get the best prices. In this book I will tell you how to get the best prices on granite. You should consider granite as it is the most asked about feature in a kitchen and most people now even demand it.

You should pick a counter type based on how you live and how the counter will be used on a daily basis. Granite is very popular. It has a very durable surface. Some require annual sealing some don't such as Home Depot has a 15 year seal. Quartz is also very popular and is very durable and easy to care for. The following shows the selection of countertops available at IKEA. It does give you an idea of matching when you put together the knobs, handles, door and drawer faces.

Sinks

Sinks look impressive in a kitchen. It is wise to get one that is double and deep. This is good for washing big pots and pans. The bowls should be about the same size. Under mount sinks are also the way to go. They are generally installed with granite or quartz counters. If you are using laminate for the counter top than a rim mounted sink is acceptable. The faucet should also match the drain and the countertop. Also a 1-hole faucet needs to match a 1 hole sink.

Faucets

Faucets need to match the countertop and the sink. You can select stainless steel or a black finish.

Dividers

IKEA has some of the best unique drawer dividers. You should make use of them. This is one of the benefits of IKEA cabinets.

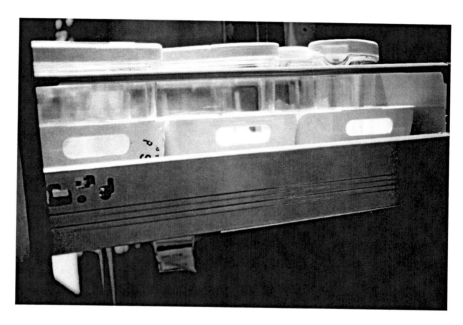

Cabinet Lighting

Under cabinet lighting is nice. It really makes cabinets look nice. I highly recommend them. Most kitchen designers also recommend them. They basically eliminate the dark shadows under the cabinets.

Backsplash

The backsplash is where you can bring a lot of life to a kitchen. There are many options available today. Glass, porcelain or marble are the way to go. When you buy the backsplash material always order 15% more than you think you need. You can then take the excess back for a refund. You need enough to cover 18 inches under the upper cabinets and 24 inches over the stove. You can order this material in square feet and it comes in boxes.

New Flooring

The kitchen floor is important as it will probably be used more than any other floor in the house. It also must complement the cabinets, counter tops and the backsplash. It must have a visual flow from the other floors leading into the kitchen. The type of kitchen floor depends on your willingness to maintain it. There are many possible options available. There is hardwood, cork, bamboo, engineered wood, stone, and porcelain.

The question is do you have an open plan and the kitchen flows into the other room then you probably need to stick with same material such as wood. It is very difficult to match two separate floors. Laminate is very good if you have a tight budget and get clickable if you want to self-install. Porcelain is available in many nice colors, does not stain, and wears hard and is easy to maintain..

Before you put anything on your floor, first get some samples and lay them out and see how they look against the cabinets.

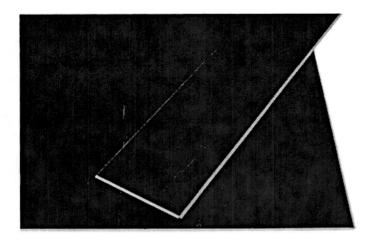

Range

If possible you should stick to the same manufacture of appliances. Since most people are now using stainless steel it is problematic as different manufactures use different finish stainless steel. If you have two appliances of different brands then it is especially noticeable. One example might be the exhaust vent and the range.

The range you pick many times makes the kitchen. You can get a nice looking GE electric stainless steel glass top range. Or you can go high end and get a high-end gas range like a Wolf.

Also you should carefully check the amperage wiring to make sure your circuit can take a new range or microwave. Many of them require more than 20 amps and may even require a dedicated circuit.

Exhaust Hood

Exhaust hoods are fashionable and serve and important purpose to remove smoke. They should be used especially above gas ranges.

Dishwasher

Try to get a very quiet dishwasher. That also helps to make a kitchen. The good ones have insulation around them to reduce sound. Some have a food grinder in them so you can put in very dirty dishes without rinsing them. Get one that has a delayed start so you can have it run later when you are sleeping.

Refrigerator

Refrigerators come in different sizes with multiple features. They can be expensive. Get one that fits your space and has all the options you think you need. They are also included in the IKEA 20% off sale. Many stores such as Sears, Home Depot and Lowes feature many sales on appliances during the year that you can take advantage of with free delivery.

DESIGN YOUR KITCHEN WITH SOFTWARE

This is a step-by-step instruction of how to design your kitchen using the IKEA 3-D software on their site.

Here are some tips to layout your kitchen:

1. Try to put the refrigerator, tall pantries, or stacked ovens at the end of the cabinet run.
2. You should always have at least 42" of space between counters. The same around islands.
3. Leave some space at the end of a cabinet run. Should be at least 1 1/2".
4. Don't put appliances next to each other. Don't put the range next the refrigerator or tall pantry. The dishwasher should also be next to the sink.
5. Use long side panels on islands. These panels are 3' x 8'. These are the same panels used next to the refrigerator.
6. When possible use cabinets with larger drawers instead of cabinets with shelves.
7. If you can keep the sink in the same location, that will save you the money for a plumber. Don't put the sink near a wall. You need some space. Don't put a sink in a corner.
8. Place upper cabinets with dishes very close to the dishwasher.
9. You should check all door swings to make sure you have the room to open the doors.

IKEA Home Planner 3D Tool

You should first do a rough sketch of your kitchen on graph paper and you should answer these questions:

a) Is this going to be a new kitchen or a remodeling of an old one?
b) Will you be expanding the kitchen space?
c) Is there access below like a basement or crawl space?
d) Is there going to be an eating place in the kitchen?
e) Do you like your current kitchen layout?
f) Why do you want to remodel?
g) Do you want a storage area in the kitchen?

Do you want to keep or replace these appliances (If you want to keep them then what are their height, width and depth?)
a) Refrigerator
b) Range
c) Dishwasher
d) Wall Oven
e) Microwave
f) Sink
g) Compactor

What kind of countertop do you want?
a) Stone
b) Formica
c) Wood
d) Granite

a) Measure full width of each wall
b) Measure windows from the floor to window sill, measure the window still to the top of the window, measure top of window to ceiling, measure from floor to ceiling and measure width of window.
c) Measure the ceiling height.

d) Floor type of construction. Is there access under the floor.

e) Does the room have soffits and are you going to remove them?

f) Are you going to change lighting?

h) Are you changing the plumbing?

i) Any change in HVACA vents or registers?

Layout

You should do rough sketches on chart paper like this one below. This is what my kitchen looked like initially on graph paper.

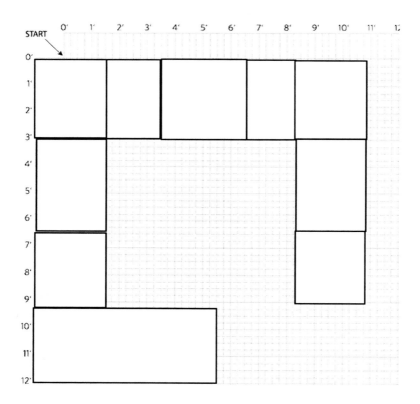

1) Now go to www.IKEA.com and click this hyperlink:
   http://www.ikea.com/ms/en_US/customer_service/IHP2_user_g
   uide/index.html

It will show you this screen:

Now click on the Quickstart button. This is a video that tells you how to use the program. All is for visual learning. No voice.

There are four sections:
1. Introduction
2. Plan Your Kitchen
3. Furnish and Decorate
4. Other Functions

Now click on Guide button and you have a video with a left menu links that tells you how to use them. All is for visual learning. No voice. You'll learn the following:

1. Interface Overview
2. Orientation
3. Menu Navigation
4. Drawing Area Color Coding
5. The Toolbar
6. Search
7. Zooming
8. Warnings
9. Login
10. Dave Your Drawing
11. Open Your Drawing
12. Print Your Drawing
13. Email Your Drawing
14. Setup Your Room

15. Furnish Your Room
16. Decorate Your Room
17. How to Order

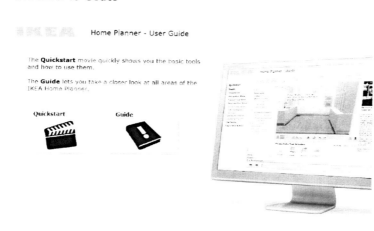

Home Planner - User Guide

The **Quickstart** movie quickly shows you the basic tools and how to use them.

The **Guide** lets you take a closer look at all areas of the IKEA Home Planner.

Quickstart   Guide

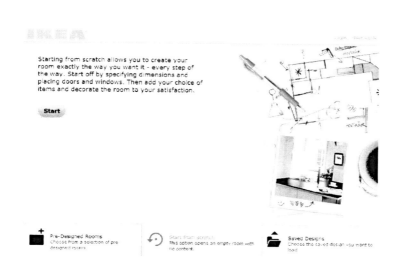

Starting from scratch allows you to create your room exactly the way you want it - every step of the way. Start off by specifying dimensions and placing doors and windows. Then add your choice of items and decorate the room to your satisfaction.

Start

Pre-Designed Rooms
Choose from a selection of pre designed rooms

Start from scratch
This option opens an empty room with no content.

Saved Designs
Choose the saved design you want to load

Here is my explanation of how to use the program: First you see this illustration:

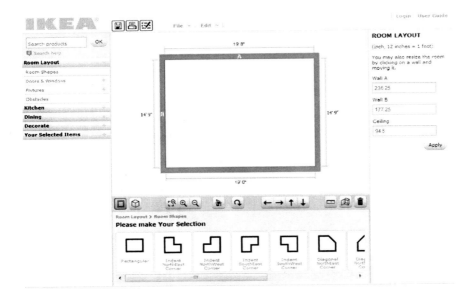

Shape of Room

The first thing to do is make your selection of the shape of the kitchen. I my case I selected the rectangular shape. See above.

Room Dimensions

Next, you need to enter the room dimensions. Wall A and B in inches. Also enter the ceiling height.

Doors

If you have doors & windows click on that. Then click on doors. Next, make your selection of the type of door. Then drag it to the room and place it where it goes. You can change handle position, door opening, frame covering and handles. You can also set the height and width in inches.

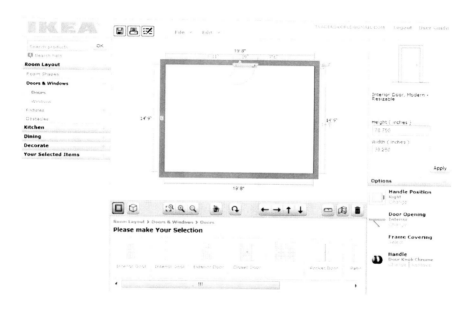

Now click windows. If you have windows make your selection and drag it onto the room and place it where it goes. Then change window background and frame covering. In the right menu set the size of the window.

If you plan to do a wall, door or window change put it in the diagram. By the way, you are looking at a big expense. If windows are going to be removed or put in then it will involve getting a city permit and possibly a zoning permit. It is best to check with a window and door company that specializes in this type of thing

You probably want the open concept as many do. It might be necessary to remove a large wall or several walls. One of the walls might be load bearing and would involve getting a structural engineer to do a drawing and have it approved by the permit office. This can easily cost $500. The drawing will specify how the roof is to be supported when the actual wall is removed. This type of change can cost from $1000 to $4000. If the wall is not load bearing then it is much easier. Just remove the drywall and framing and any electrical wires.

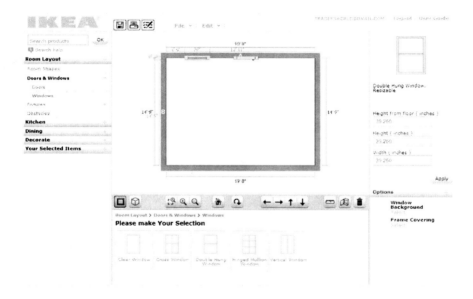

Fixtures – Plumbing & Gas Pipes

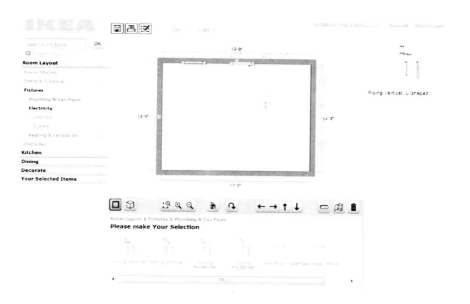

Next click fixtures and then click plumbing & gas pipes. Place those where they go in the room.

It is important that you should use licensed and insured plumbers and electricians. Their work will then comply with your local building codes. This is for your safety. It is not worth it to hire unlicensed trade people as you might risk the safety of your home. You need to take those costs into account also.

When you remove the old cabinets, you will probably need to change the plumbing. Your sink location will change. The refrigerator will probably change and will the water line to the icemaker. Old valves need to be changed to new ones. In most cases a licensed plumber will be necessary. If you are planning to move a sink, then make sure from a plumber that it is possible. Check the risers and drainage pipes to make sure it is possible. Same with gas lines, check to make sure it is possible to move them.

If you are buying a brand new oven, it might take more electrical power than your old oven, so you should ask questions from an electrician and have him take a look and ask him to advise you.

Electrical - Switches

Next click Electricity and then switches.

Place those where they go in the diagram.

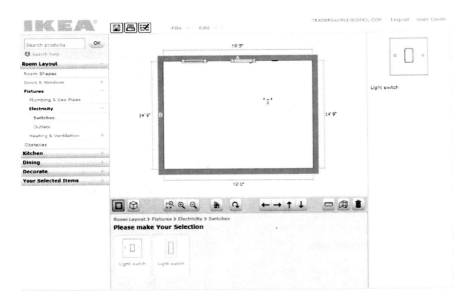

Electrical – Outlets

Then click outlets. Place them where they go in the room.

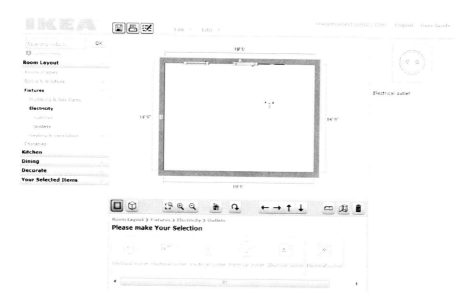

Heating and Ventilation

Now click heating and ventilation. Click if you have any of these items in the room and drag them to their places. This includes radiators, air conditioners, vents, fireplaces and free standing heater stoves.

Obstacles

Next click obstacles. Drag any of these into the room such as floor obstacles, posts, columns, partition walls, ceiling boxes, sloping ceilings, soffits, resizable and glass partitions. You can, of course, change the width and depth in inches of any of these obstacles.

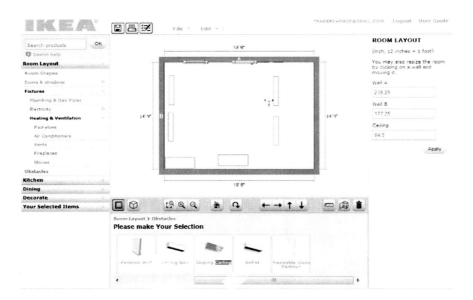

Built-in Kitchens – Base Cabinets

Next click kitchen. Then click on built-in kitchens. Then click base cabinets. You have an excellent selection of anything you could possibly want. Drag and drop the base cabinets where you want them in the room.

1) For sink
2) For oven
3) For cook top
4) With drawers
5) With shelves
6) With wire baskets
7) With pull-out functions
8) With open end shelves
9) With open shelves

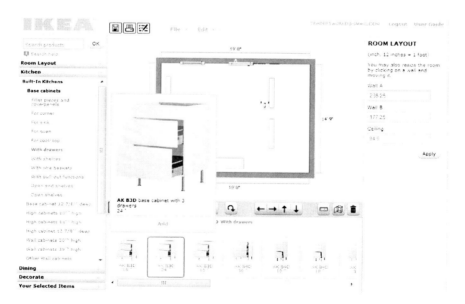

High Cabinets

Next click high cabinets if you have no soffits. There are two selections:

80" high

88" high.

Which one you use depends on how high your ceilings are.

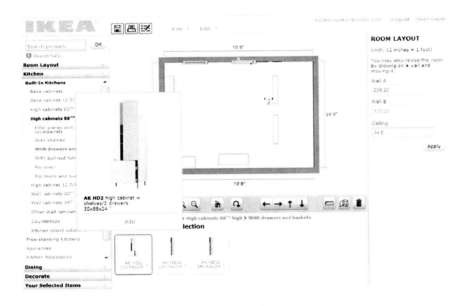

Wall Cabinets

Now click on the wall cabinets to pull those illustrations up. There are two heights. 30" if you have soffits and 39" if you have no soffits. You will see:

1) For corner
2) With doors
3) With glass doors
4) For microwave
5) Open shelves

You can drag them to the room and position them where they should go.

Generally if have a 30" base cabinet selected for the kitchen, then you should have a 30" wall cabinet to match it. They should in fact line up right on top of each other.

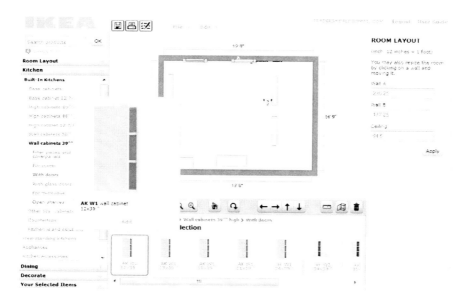

Other Wall Cabinets

Now select other wall cabinets. There you can select

1) Fan cabinets
2) Top cabinets for fridge/freezers
3) Horizontal cabinets
4) Roll-front cabinets
5) Open wall shelves

Now drag and drop any of those where you want them.

Next click countertops and you will see

1) Extra countertop solutions
2) Corner countertop solutions

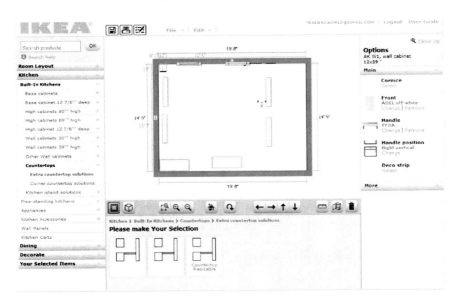

Select any of those that apply to you.

Kitchen Island Solutions

Now click kitchen island solutions

Select either Akurum solutions or stand-alone solutions if you want an island.

Kitchen islands are very popular and add a lot of value to a kitchen. You have extra workspace and convenient seating. The normal cabinet is 24" wide and if you add seating to it you would add another 12" to the countertop making the countertop 36".

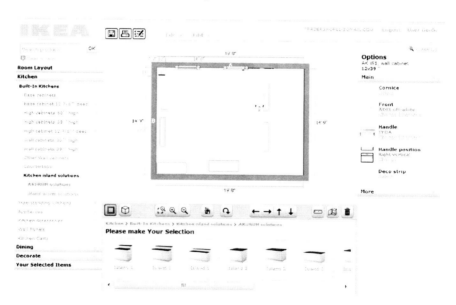

Appliances

Next select appliances and you will see:

1) Range
2) Dishwashers
3) Fridge/Freezer
4) Extractor Hoods
5) Your own appliances

Select those that apply to you and drag them into the room.

Dining

Now select dining. You will see:

1) Dining tables
2) Dining Chairs
3) Bar tables
4) Stools and benches
5) Dining sets
6) Cabinets and sideboards

Select and drag any of those that apply to you.

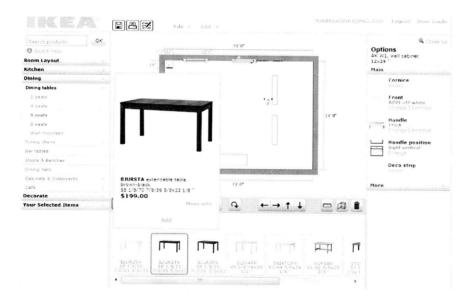

Decorate

Now select decorate. Then choose Group Options:

1) Counter tops
2) Wall edge strips
3) Legs /Toe Kicks
4) Handles
5) Cornices
6) Deco Strips

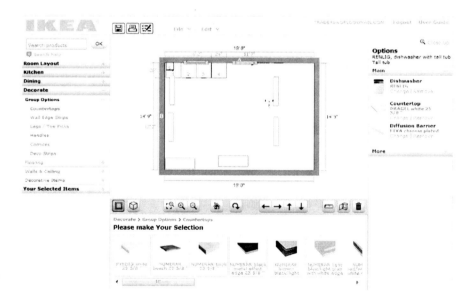

Flooring

Next choose flooring and then select:

1) Wood
2) Tile
3) Stone
4) Granite
5) Carpeting
6) IKEA Flooring

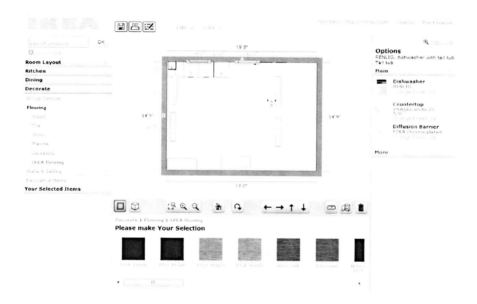

Walls and Ceiling

Next select walls and ceiling and select:

1) Walls
2) Ceilings
3) Moldings
4) Molding Trim and Skirting

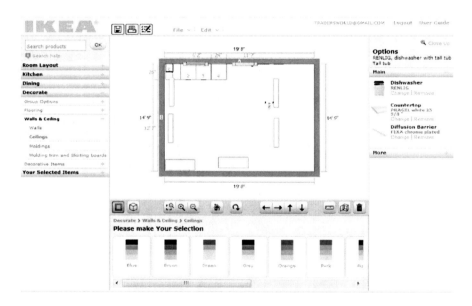

Select those selections that apply to you.

Save File

Next go up to file and save it with a name. You then see your saved design and it should look like this. Before you can save it you will need to register for an account. It will ask you for a username and password.

Your saved designs

kitchen9ap (v9)
8/1/2013 12:55:15 PM
Big without counter tops

Pre-Designed Rooms
Choose from a selection of pre-designed rooms.

Start from scratch
This option opens an empty room with no content.

Saved Designs
Choose the saved design you want to load.

Open Saved File

Now click the file on the saved designs to pull up your designed kitchen.

There are two ways to view it. One is 2D and the other is 3D.

Here is the illustration of my kitchen I designed in 3D. You don't see counter tops as I got them from Home Depot. Also you don't see the panels on the islands or beside the dishwasher as those are not configurable.

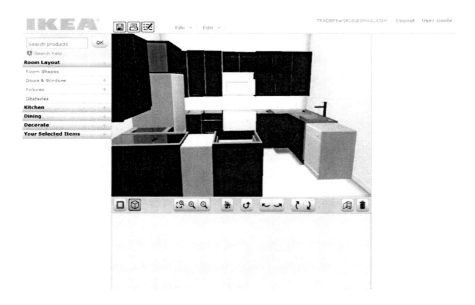

Here is my kitchen is in 2D format.

Cabinet Doors and Drawers

When you click on any cabinet you can change the type of doors you want. My cabinet doors and drawers selected were the PERFEKT RAMSJO type. You can select to add or remove a cornice, front, handle, handle position and deco strip.

Also by clicking any of the buttons on the bottom tab you can change the view of the kitchen at many different angles.

Again in my illustration I did not include countertops as I was having a 3rd party locally install them, namely Home Depot. Also I did not show panels for the sides of the refrigerator, dishwasher, or the cabinet with the trash compactor as you can't illustrate them in this software. They also have to be cut for each particular case.

Your Selected Items

Now if you click on your selected items on the left side it will show everything in your order and its illustration and price and a total. When you are ready to order your cabinets just give an IKEA kitchen department person your username and password and they can pull up your order and you can place it. Ask them you go over the plan and make sure there are no mistakes and anything that they would recommend changed. Then after they finish reviewing the plan and have given to OK place the order. Also ask them if everything is in stock.

After the order is placed the stockroom can usually pull together your entire order usually in two hours.

Delivery

You will need a truck to pick up your order. If you have ordered any of the 3' X 8' panels you will need to have a larger truck that can carry that size of panel. If you live near IKEA then you are lucky as the whole order can then be delivered to you and you can eliminate that problem.

Laying out Cabinets with tape

I found it helpful to layout the kitchen cabinets with blue tape on the floor. Then I could get a feeling of what the kitchen will be like. It also helps to confirm if the electrical switches and sockets are in the right place as well as plumbing. I also used old CDs on the floor to indicate where the recessed light would be in the ceiling above. By the way recessed lighting should be 3 feet apart and at the edge of the cabinets.

INSTALLING THE KITCHEN

1. Clear a Space

Make sure you have a cleared space on the perimeter for workers to do their job. Is there room for their tools? Is there enough room to assemble the cabinets and place to put them before they go into the kitchen area?

Empty all old kitchen cabinets and put the materials into boxes and take them out of the work area! This is a must! Dust will go everywhere and you don't want to have to clean dust off of everything you had in the old cabinets

2. Tips for setting up your upper cabinets

1. If you know where all of your base cabinets go then it is easy to setup your upper cabinets. Just merely align them with the base cabinets. For example, a 30" wide base cabinet should have a 30" upper cabinet. If possible they should also have the same size doors.
2. The upper cabinets need to be around 17" – 19" above the counter top. However there should be 24" – 30" above the stove. You should check your local codes on this. This is, of course, for fire safety. Also consider a hood vent or a microwave with a built in vent.
3. You should also leave space for side panels both sides of the vent or microwave. Panels also will go on the ends of the upper cabinet runs.
4. Leave clearance at the end of the cabinet runs approximately 1 ½" so the doors can open correctly.
5. Put a cover panel between the refrigerator and the cabinets next to it so you won't have to see the side of it. It looks more

finished and built in. IKEA sells panels that at 3' x 8' designed for this.

3. Assembling the IKEA Cabinets

The cabinets should be assembled on a soft surface so they don't get scratched. Carpet is excellent for this purpose. IKEA gives you excellent visual instructions how to assemble both the base and upper cabinets. After you do one of each it is extremely easy. These cabinets are engineered nearly perfect. Everything fits together exactly and there are no missing parts! You should assemble all the base units and then the upper units.

5. Tools You Will Need

You will need a hammer, wrench, knife, drill bits, screwdriver bits, gloves, tape measure, and a level.

I used a round sorter and dumped the screws in separate slots to keep them organized. You should read the IKEA cabinet assembly instructions carefully and take your time and you'll find the cabinets are easy to put together. Once you put your first one together the rest are easy. They just take time.

Wall Cabinets Instructions

Where to start?

The wall cabinets should be what you start on first in your kitchen remake project.

First as I said before, find a good place you can assemble them. Preferably I would recommend that you build them on a carpet. That is what I did and it work nicely. That will prevent the cabinets from getting scratched or the corners getting damaged. They will come in different sizes. When they are fully assembled, I would then place them where they go in the kitchen.

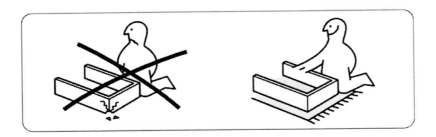

The following is the carpet that I used to assemble the cabinets. Place the cabinet components on the carpet. Then read the instructions carefully as you assemble and screw them together. Take your time and do it right.

It is wise to get help putting the cabinets together and especially carrying the cabinets to the kitchen. You don't want to injure yourself or the cabinets lifting them. I would recommend at least two people.

If you need help and don't understand the instructions you can always call IKEA and ask them questions about the assembly. I called them several times and they were very helpful. When calling ask for the kitchen department and someone their can help you.

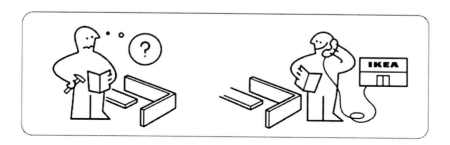

These are the parts that come in the boxes. You'll get complete instructions, just visual. They don't come with text instructions. Before you start assembling the cabinets make sure you have all the parts and know about where they go from the illustrations. I have found virtually no missing parts in the cabinets that I assembled.

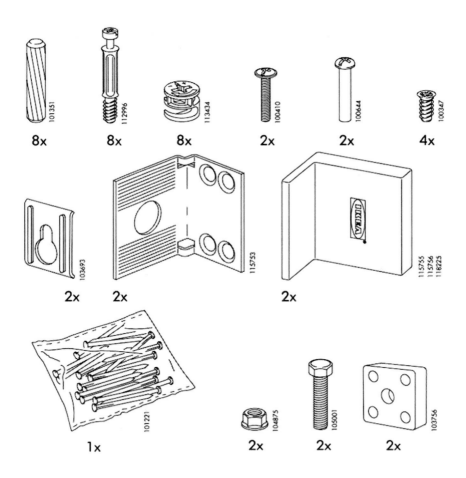

Don't put the doors on the cabinets until they are in the kitchen and mounted to the walls. There again it is very important that you don't injure yourself or the cabinets. Take your time following the instructions carefully and you will be awarded a fantastic kitchen.

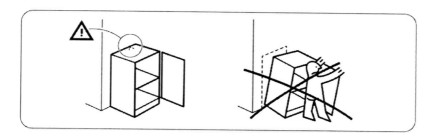

First place the side panels on the carpeted floor or on a rug. Then screw in the L brackets with the 2x screws using a Philips screwdriver. Notice that the groove on the side panel is on the same side as the bracket.

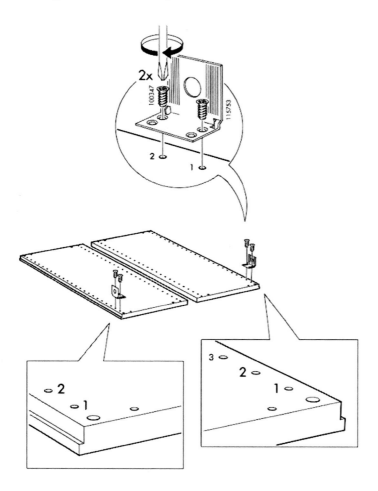

Next put the 8x screws in.

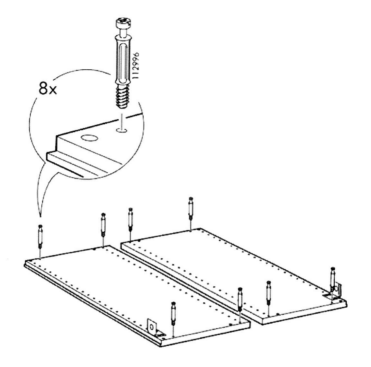

Next put the 4x wood dowels in and side the panels as illustrated.

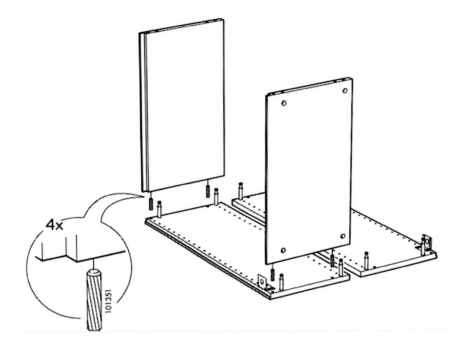

Now put the 8x short metal cam screws in.

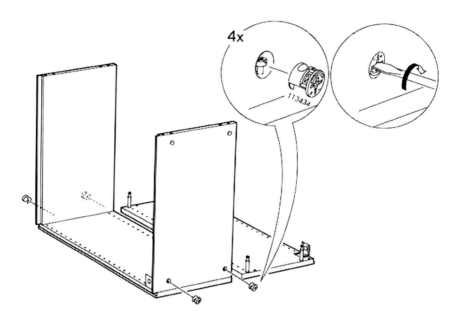

Next put the next panel on using the 4x wood dowels.

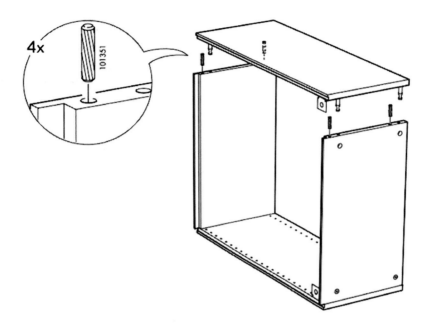

Screw in the 4x metal screws.

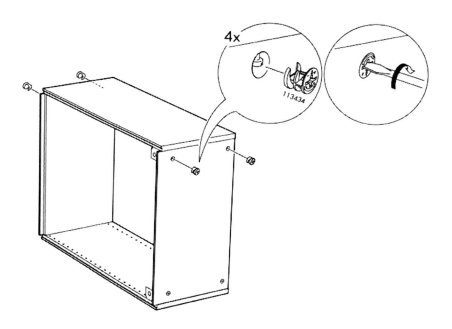

Now put the back on and nail it securely to the box.

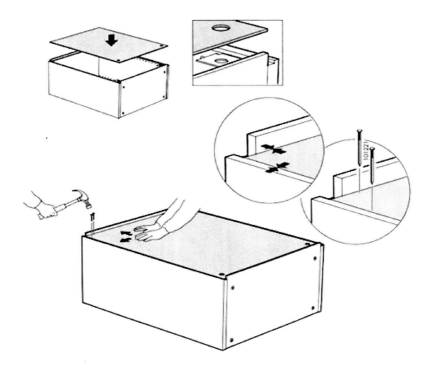

Now it can be placed in the kitchen where it goes.

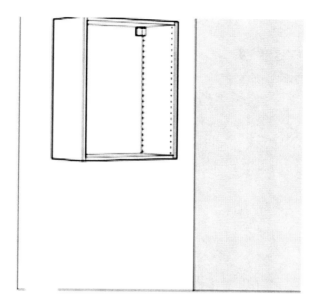

The upper cabinets should be hung on the rail. The rail should be cut to the length of the wall so the cabinets can be hung on them. Use a level so the cabinets will be level. You'll need heavy duty 2 ½" builder screws that go into the wall joists as they will need to hold very heavy cabinets.

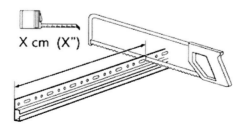

X cm (X")

Notice where the rail is mounted in this picture of my kitchen and that is where your rail should be placed. Make sure the rail is level and secured with construction heavy duty screws directly into the wall joists.

The cabinets are hung on the rails using the metal corner brackets on the rear top of the cabinets.

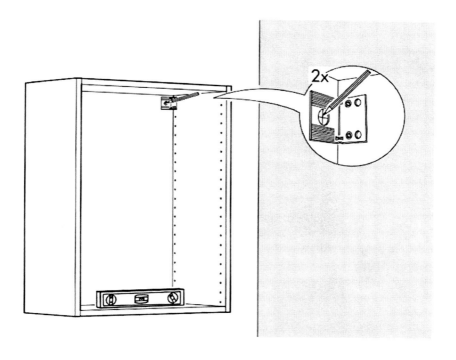

The rails are hung near the top of the wall using construction screws that go into the wall joists.

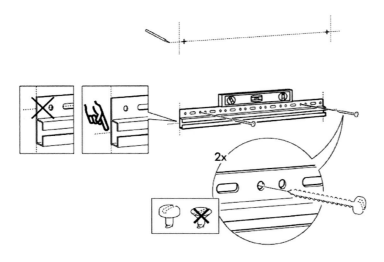

Then the 2x screws with a sliding bracket are inserted into the rail and slid over to where the cabinet goes.

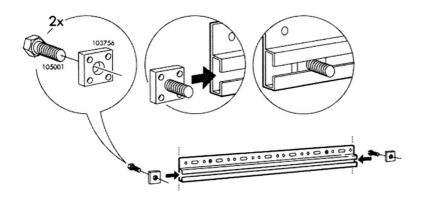

Then the cabinet goes on to the screws and is secured with a nut using a crescent wrench.

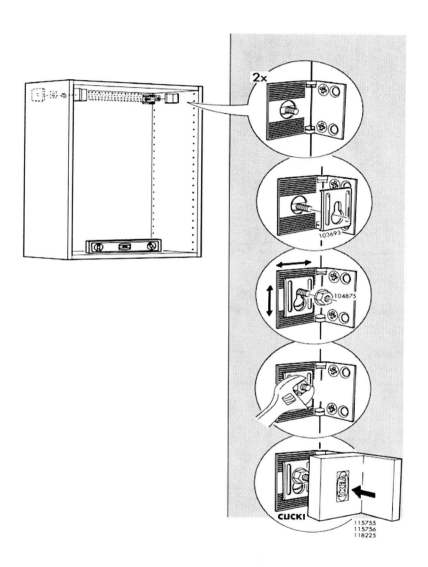

Use clamps to hold the cabinets together.

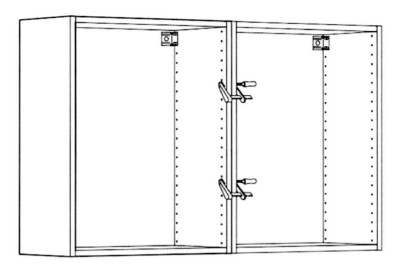

Then drill holes through and insert provided screws to tie the cabinets together.

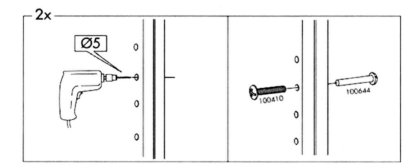

This is that the cabinets look like after they are mounted on the rails.

This is what the cabinets look like after the doors are mounted on to the base cabinets.

This is an inside look at the shelves and how much the sheves can hold.

Here is another upper cabinet.

See the organization using IKEA plate holders.

Base Cabinets with Shelves Instructions

The base cabinets are the next step. This is what they look like after assembly. These are the foundation of the entire kitchen. They go on the floor.

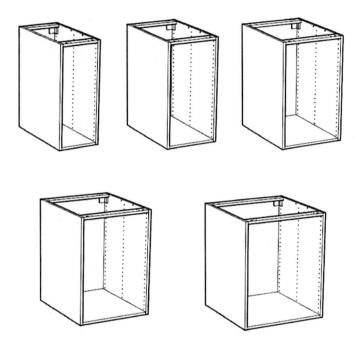

Use the same tools at you used on the wall cabinets.

These are the included screws, brackets, etc. that come with each cabinet.

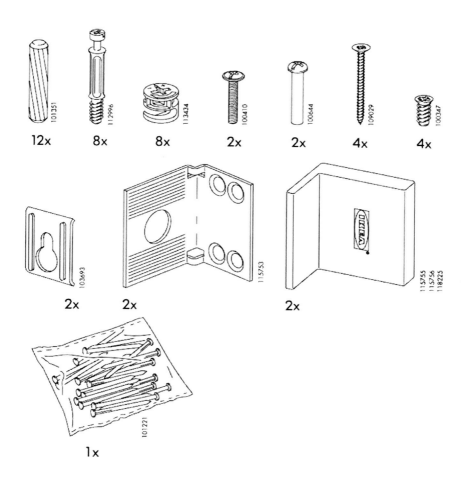

Lay out the two panels as show in the picture below. Then put the brackets on using the 2x screws.

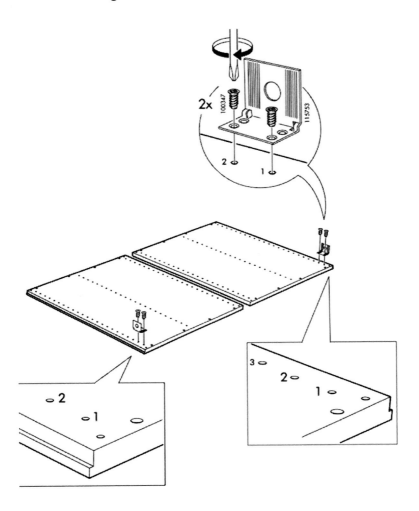

Next put the 8x screws in.

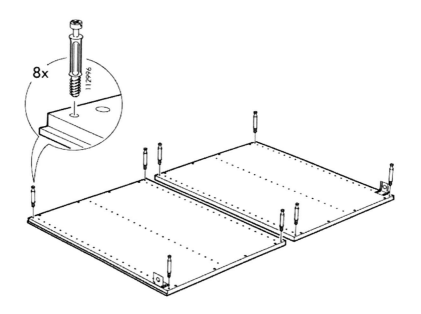

Now insert the panels as show below using the 6x wood dowels.

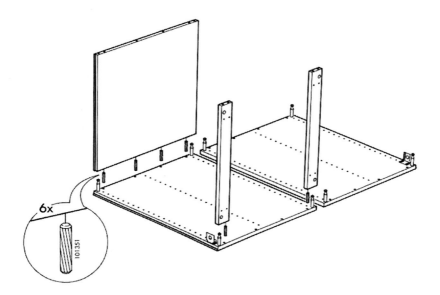

Now secure them using the 4x screws.

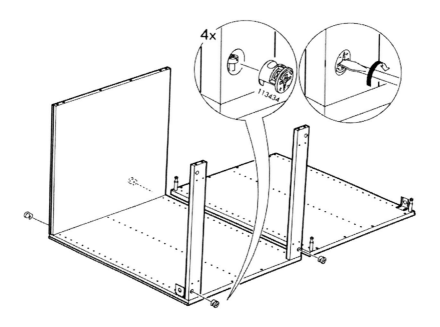

Now use the 6x wood dowels and attach the next panel.

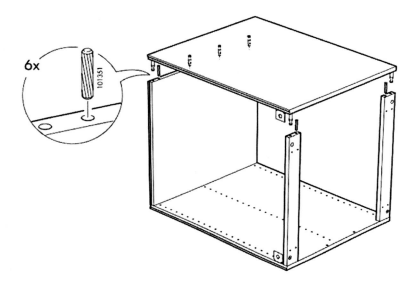

Now use the 4x screws to secure them.

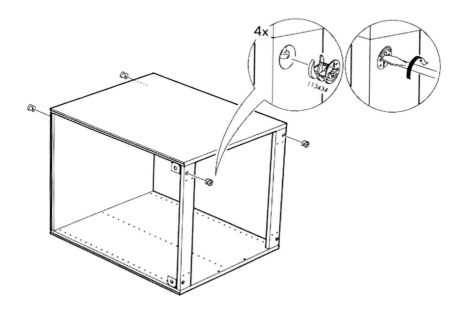

Now insert the back panel.

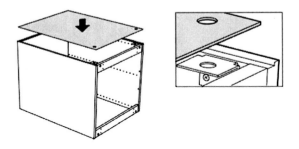

Nail it on using the small nails and a hammer.

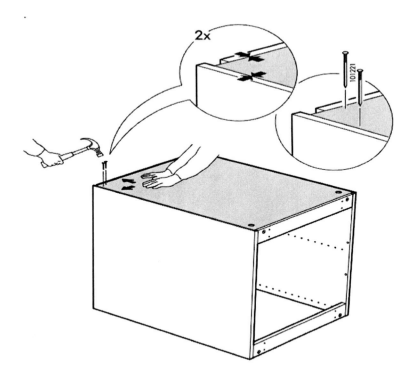

Now nail each corner.

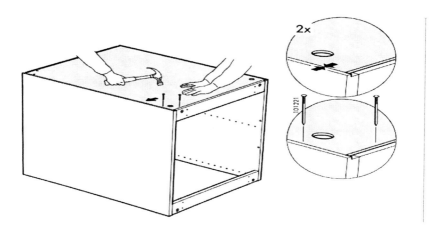

Now use all of the nails provided.

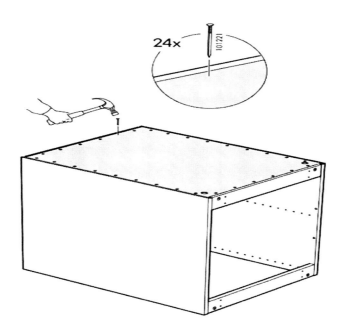

Now place the legs on the cabinets.

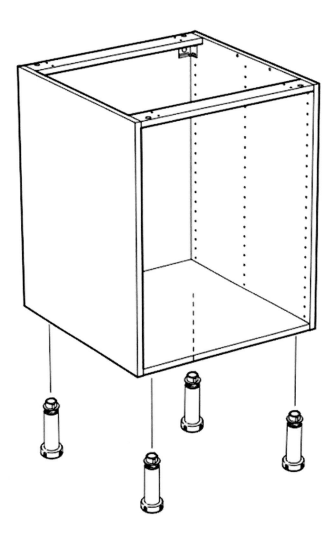

This is what the legs look like. See the next section on legs.

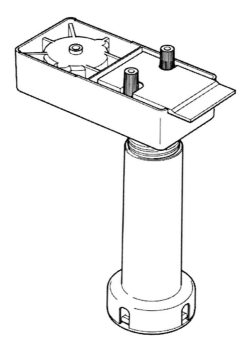

The cabinets need to be secured to the wall so they don't fall over.

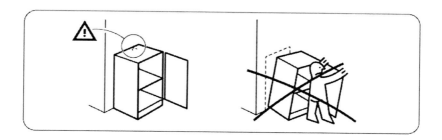

Make sure the cabinets are level. Then mark the wall where the screw goes.

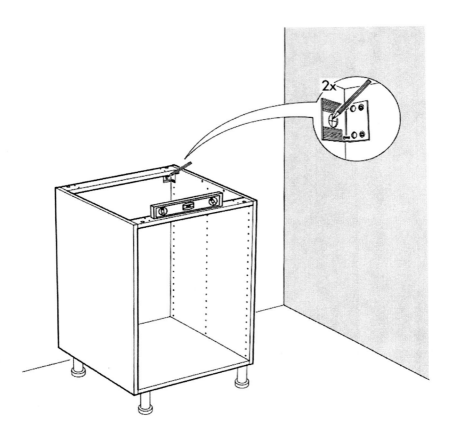

Now put the screws in.

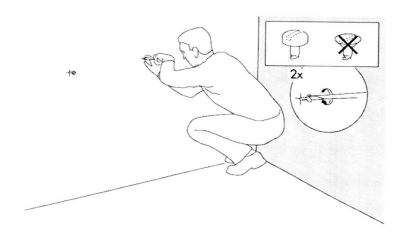

Now put the cabinets back. Tighten up the screws as shown.

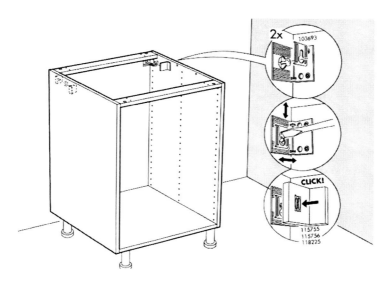

Use clamps to tie cabinets together.

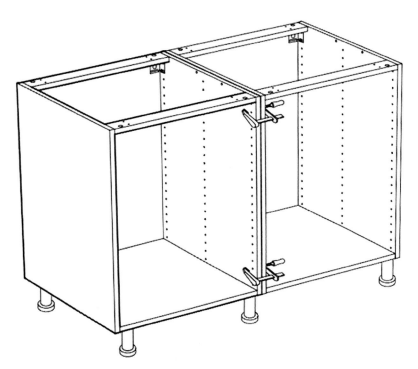

Now use screws to tie the cabinets together.

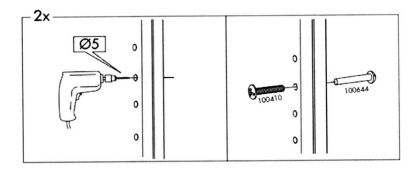

If you are using IKEA countertops now is the time to put them on.

Using the screws provided.

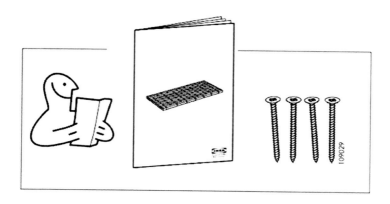

This is what the under sink cabinet looks like.

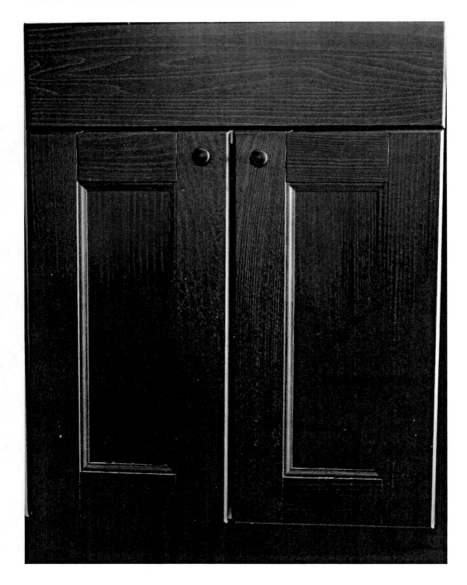

This is the organization under the sink.

Installing the Cabinet Legs

Here are the parts to the legs.

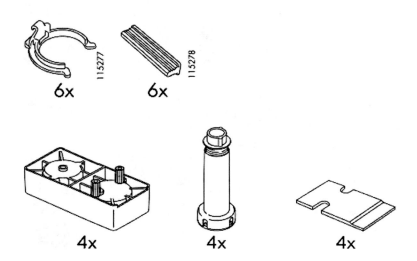

This is what the legs look like when assembled. They go under the base cabinets with the predrilled holes.

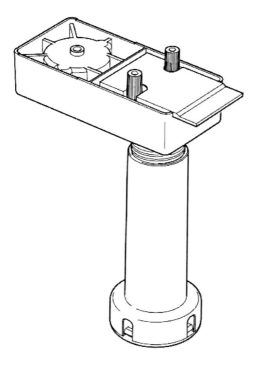

This is an illustration how to mount the legs.

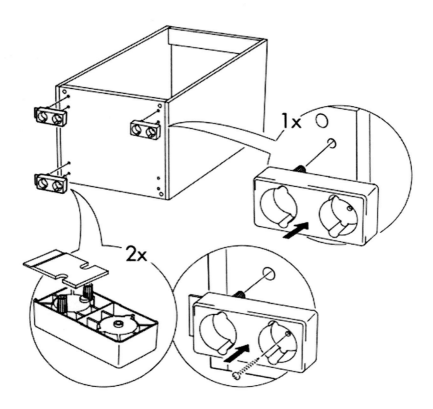

Again be careful you need two people to turn the cabinets back upright as if not done correctly you will break the legs.

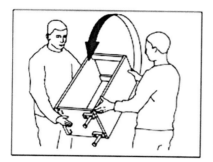 

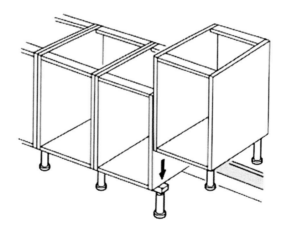

This is how to connect to the kick plate.

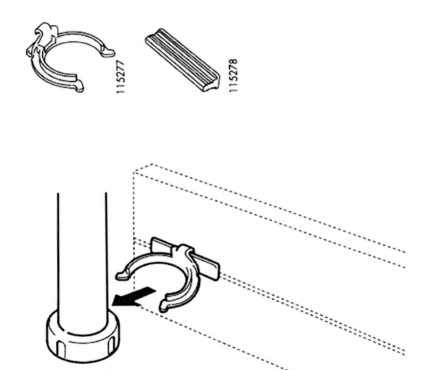

The cabinets can be leveled by just adjusting each leg. Or one nice way to level the base cabinets is the put a 1x4 inch board on the wall and level it. Place the back of the cabinets on the 1x4 board. Then use the front legs to level the front of the cabinets. This saves the time of having to level both the back and front legs.

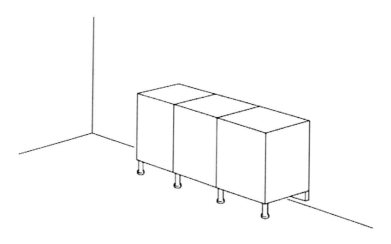

Not a good idea to put legs on all cabinets corners as show. It is then impossible to level them.

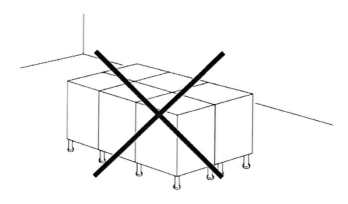

If you don't use the back leveling board it is ok to use legs on the front of the cabinets and then just a leg on the back ends as shown here.

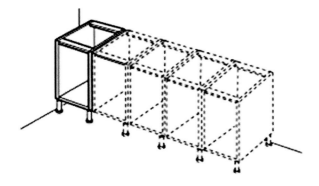

The final set of cabinets should look like this.

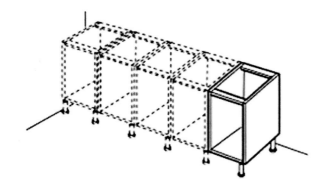

.

Also be careful when moving the cabinets. It is best to have two people and to lift the cabinet before moving or you will break the legs.

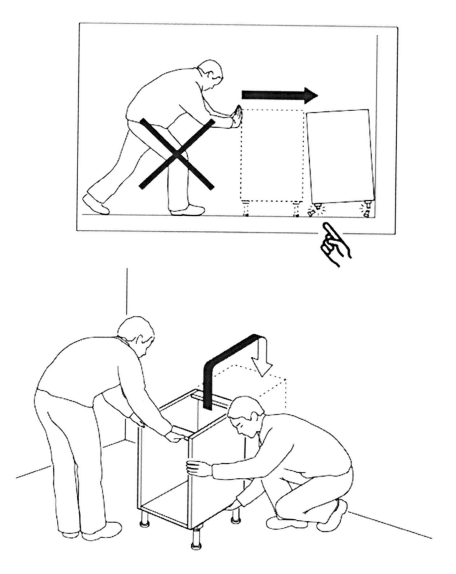

Assembling the Drawers in the Base Cabinets

Here are the instructions to assemble the base cabinets with drawers. I personally found these cabinets to be my favorite. The more you have of these the better you will like them. Try to configure as many of these as possible into your kitchen.

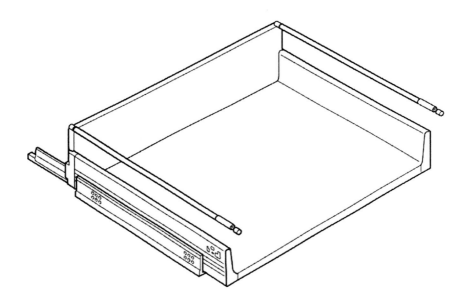

First put the rails in the cabinets and screw them in using the 2x screws.

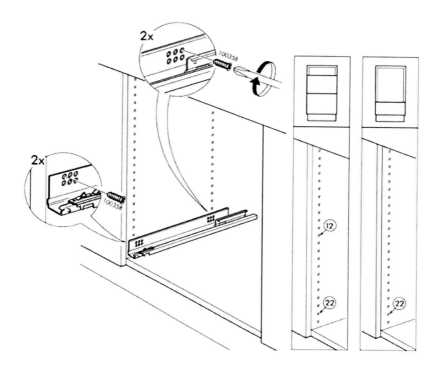

Next put the drawers together with a click.

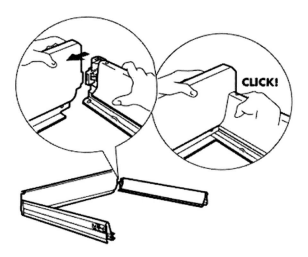

Next slide the bottom panel in.

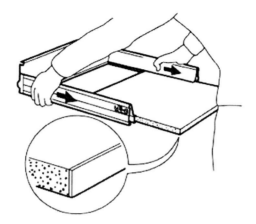

Next screw the door brackets in.

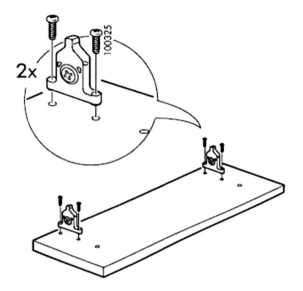

Next put the door bumpers on.

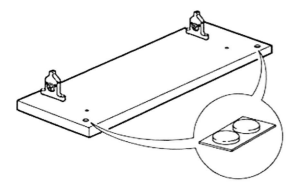

Now click the front on.

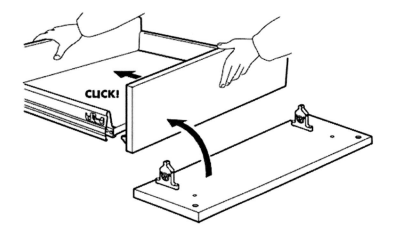

Next put the rod on.

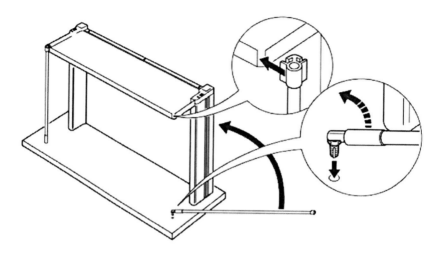

Next the IKEA name plate.

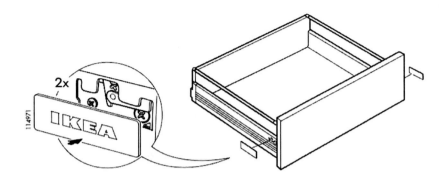

Now slide the doors in.

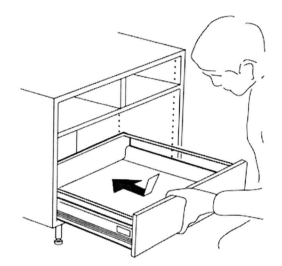

The doors can be adjusted two ways. This is one way.

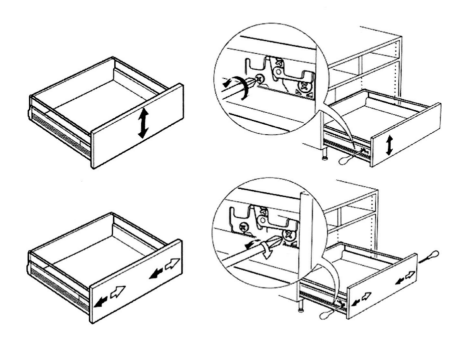

This is the other way.

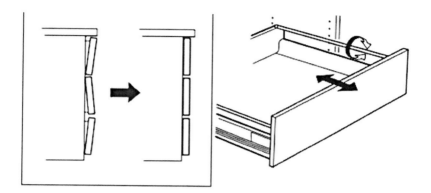

The take the doors out just pull out and lift up.

This is that the cabinet looks like after assembled.

This is what the inside of the doors looks like with IKEA organization accessories for silverware.

This is the inside the doors with IKEA organization accessories for plates and bowls.

Corner Base Cabinets

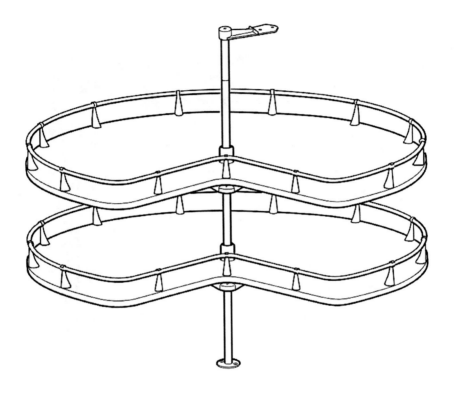

These are the parts needed to put the corner cabinets together.

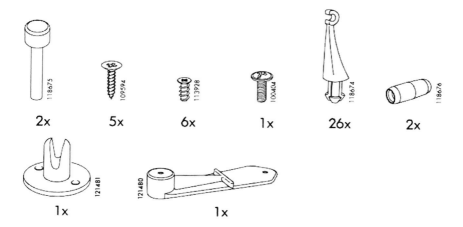

First install the wire in the cabinet.

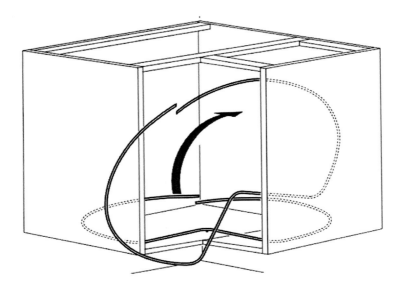

Next screw the bracket on the turn table.

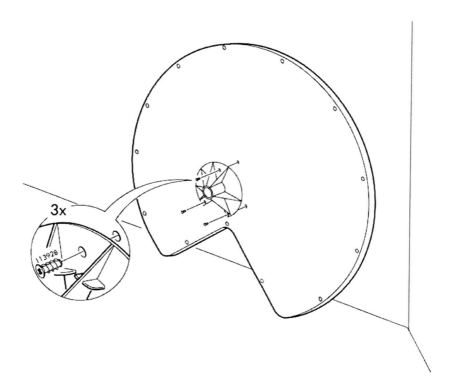

Next step install the bracket.

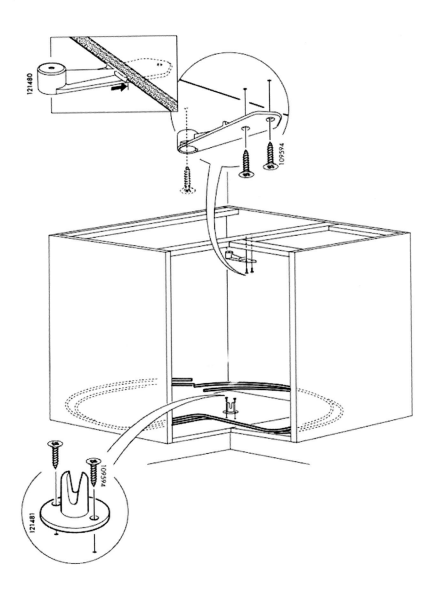

Next step put the round shelves in.

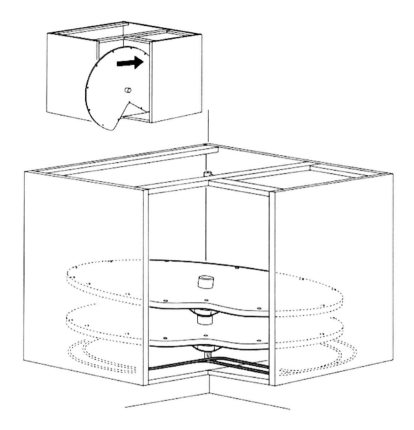

Now put the rod together.

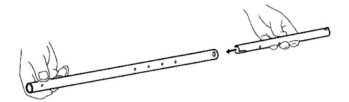

Now slide the rod in.

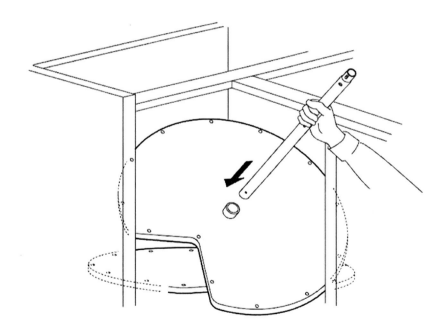

Next step put it all together.

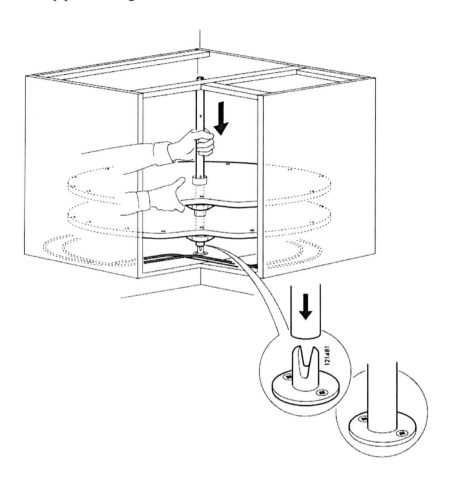

Next put the screw in the rod to secure it.

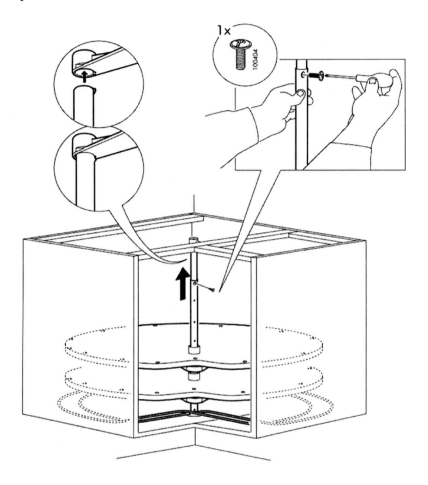

Now screw the bottom in.

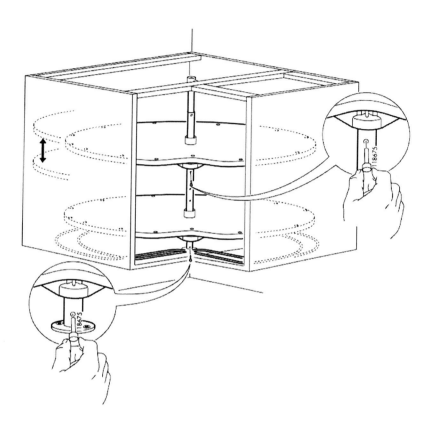

Now put the rail clips in.

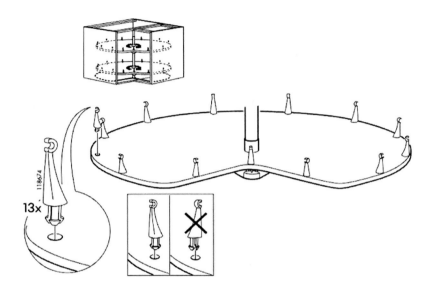

Now put the rail in.

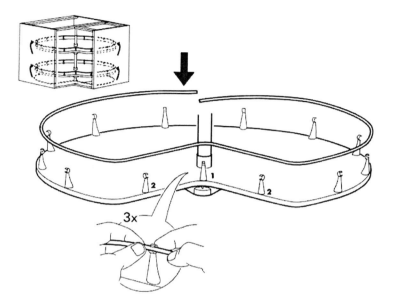

Now secure it.

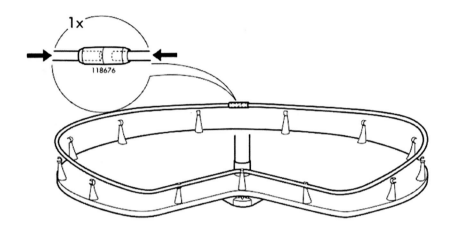

Clip the rail in and you are done.

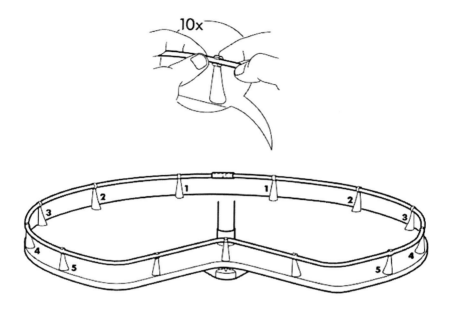

This is what the outside of a corner cabinets look like.

This is what the inside looks like. As you can see it holds a lot.

High Cabinets

Here are the high cabinets which are about the same as the base cabinets. Generally used beside the refrigerator and end of cabinets. I did not configure them in our kitchen as I did not have the room.

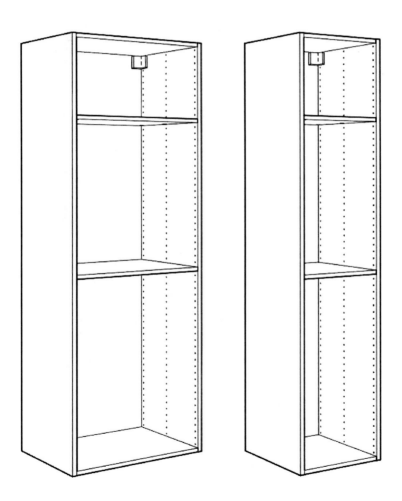

Here are the parts needed.

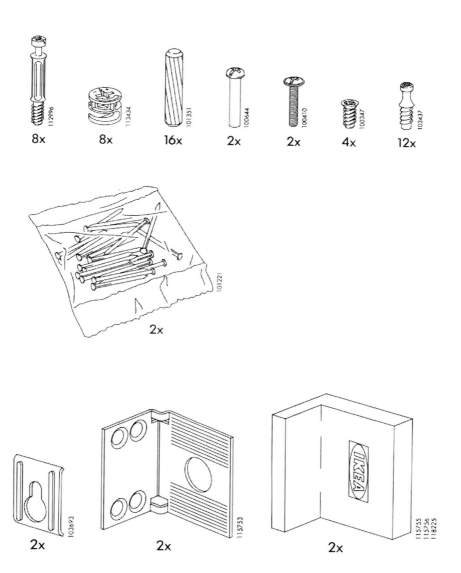

Put the side panels down on the rug or carpet and insert the 12x screws.

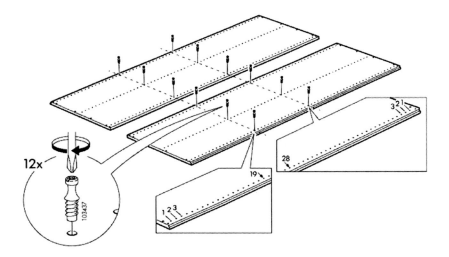

Now screw the brackets in.

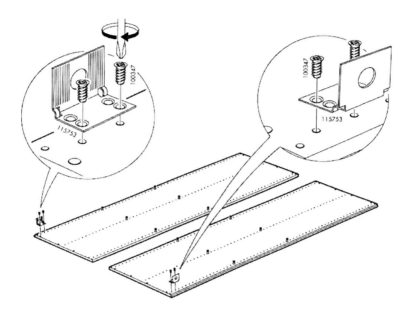

Insert the 8x screws into the panels.

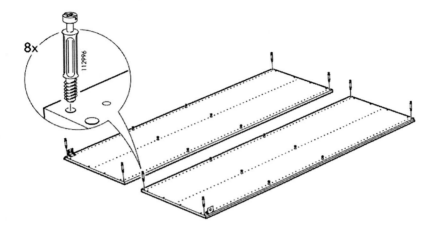

Now put these panels in using the 8x wood dowels.

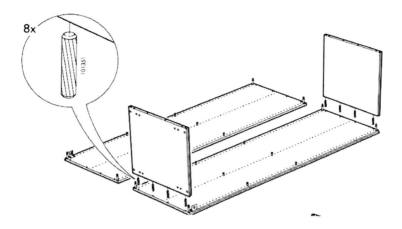

And now put the 4x screws in.

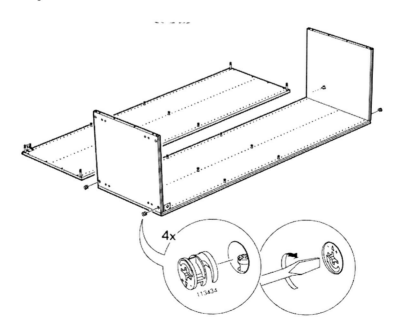

Now put the next panel in using the 8x wood dowels.

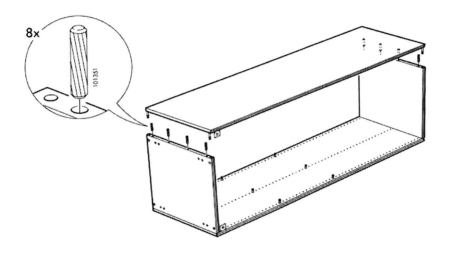

And now put the 4x screws in.

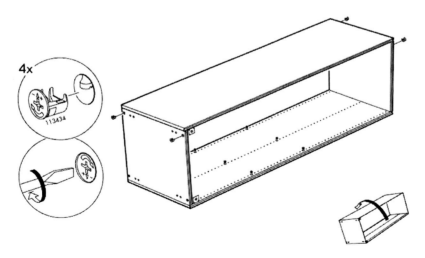

Now put the back panel on and nail it on.

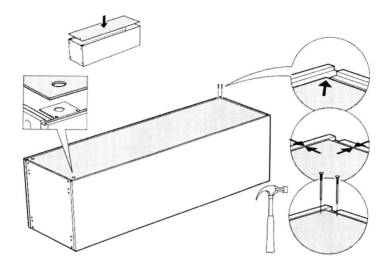

Now put the rest of the nails in.

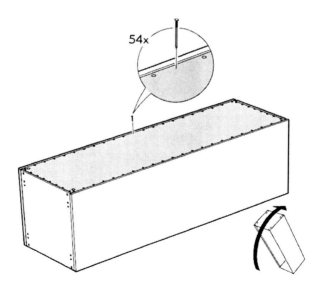

Now put the legs on.

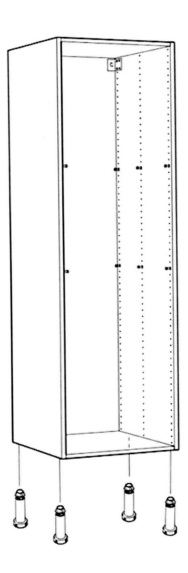

Now level it and screw it to the wall.

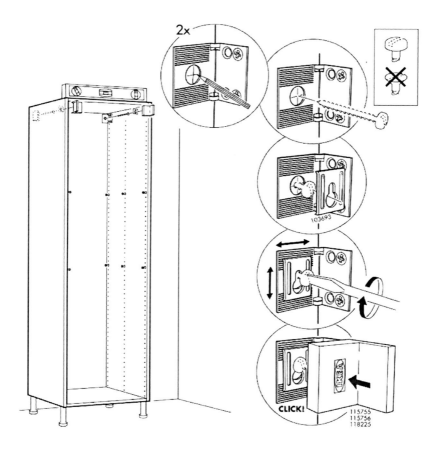

Now put the shelves in.

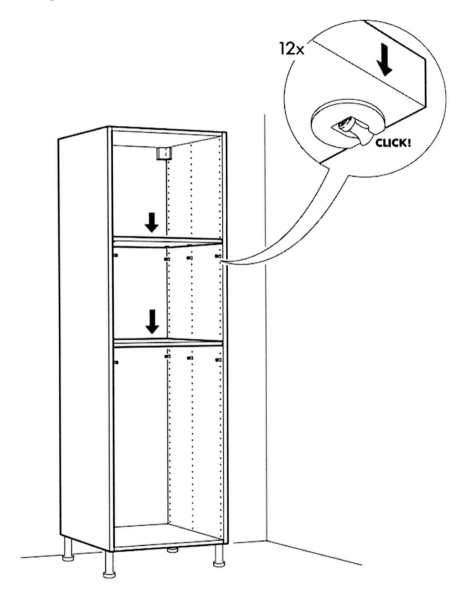

Now if you have more than one unit tie them together the same way as you did with the base and wall cabinets. That is first using clamps and then drilling the holes and inserting the screws to hold them together. Don't forget to use the level.

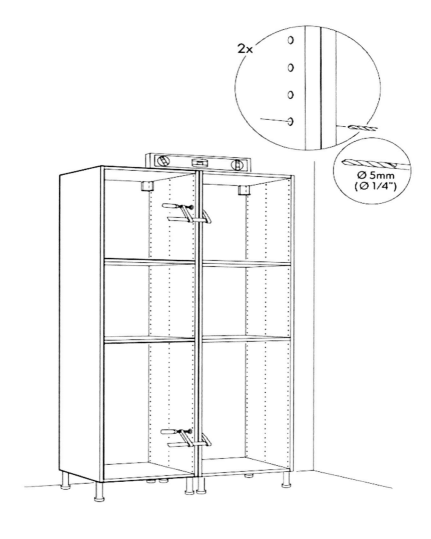

Use brackets and provided screws and you are done.

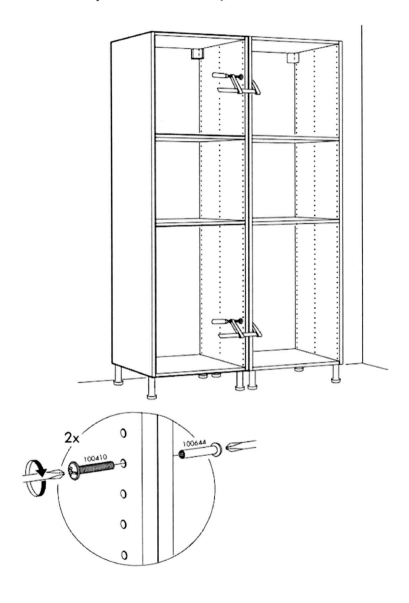

Putting a Dishwasher in at the end of Cabinets

To put an appliance in at the end of the cabinets you will need to build a cabinet manually using either plywood or using the IKEA panels. I used plywood for the box and used an IKEA panel for the fronts and the end. Here is the construction of the box using plywood. I used brackets to hold it together. See the water tube going to the garbage disposal from the dishwasher.

I used part of a panel for the front. I drilled holes for the electrical and the water tube going to the dishwasher from the garbage disposal.

Use iron on wood to cover cuts where they were exposed by the saw.

This is what the IKEA end panel looks like when finished. It looks very nice and professional in my opinion.

Attach the Panels to the Islands

Next attach the panels to the islands. It is OK to have the grain run sideways. You have to cut a panel the same way for the refrigerator.

To make sure you the cut is straight use the T-guide that is on most Skill saws. Better yet use a table saw if you have one. I did not have one, so I just used the skill saw.

Refrigerator Panels

Now it is time to cut and attach the refrigerator panels. This will give the kitchen a finished look.

Measure the width of the panels so it will cover the sides of the refrigerator. In my case the sides were gray and did not look that good in this kitchen. Also measure the height to the top of the cabinets.

To cut the side panel I would again recommend using a skill saw with a laser guide and a T-square guide. Measure it accurately with a tape measure. Using the Skill Saw built in T-square will give you a perfect straight cut. Use a high end blade with a fine cut (that means a large number of cutting teeth).

Cabinet Above the Refrigerator

The refrigerator does not look good with the cabinet above it. As you can see the cabinet is back too far. The cabinet needs to be moved forward. You need to pull it to the front and then secure it with at least 6 – 8 screws into the side panels. See the next picture where I moved to cabinet to the front. Some recommend building a box on its rear to support the cabinet. I did not feel that it was necessary. If you feel it necessary then build and install the rear box and then screw back of the cabinet onto the box.

Now the cabinet has been moved forward and looks nice as it should.

Toe Kick

The toe kick goes on the bottom of the cabinets.

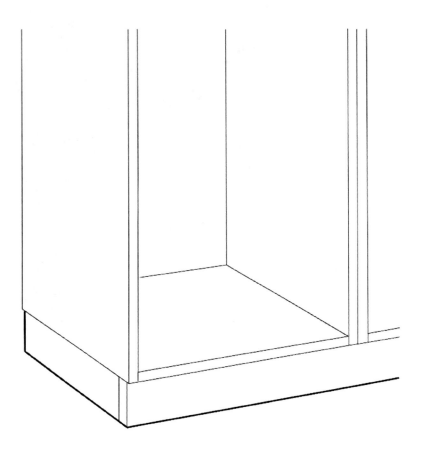

The toekick can be cut square or with an angle in the corners. I just used the square cut.

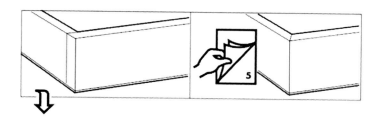

Measure the cabinets by pushing the boards in like this.

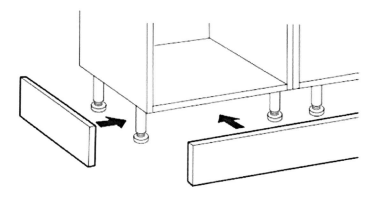

If you use the square cut you will need to iron on wood at the ends.

If you use angle cuts then no ironing is needed.

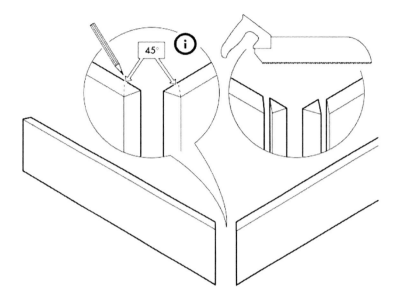

Glue on the protective plastic on the bottoms of the boards. This is to prevent ruining the boards just in case the floor gets wet.

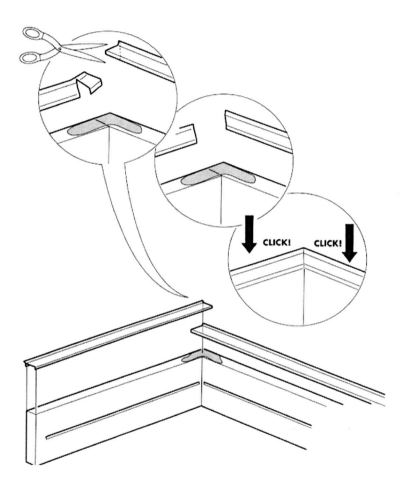

Insert the plastic strips into the boards and hammer them in.

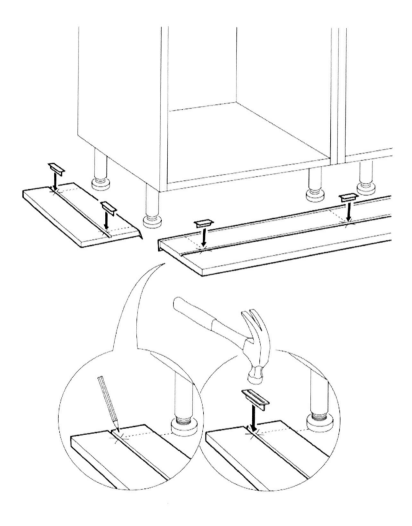

Now insert the leg holders.

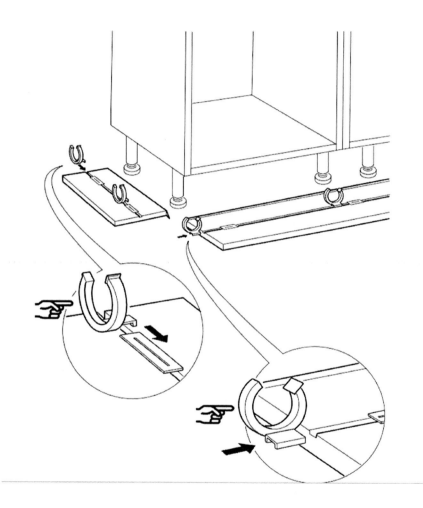

Now attach the boards to the legs and you are done.

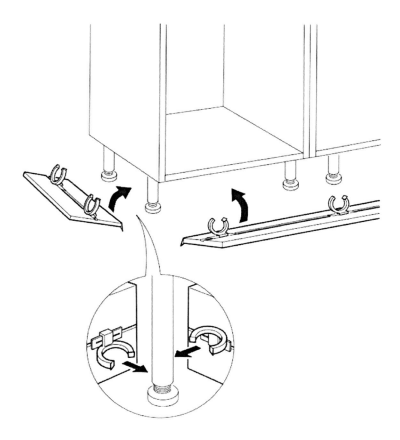

This is what the toe kick looks like after installed. Notice I continued it all the way under the dishwasher. That gives it a cleaner look than having the black toe kick that comes with most dishwashers.

Cabinet Side Panel

The cabinet side panels should be screwed to the sides of the cabinets. Use a clamp to hold it in place before screwing.

Molding Installation and Cutting Instructions

I prefer using a power saw miter cutter. It saves a lot of time.

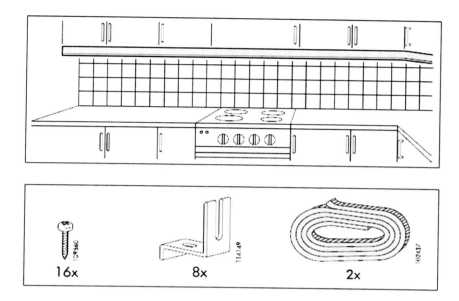

There are several ways to install the molding. See the illustration above. This is one way and the most common. Use the 8x L-brackets and 16x screws to attach them to the bottom of the cabinets. Use these angles for the cutting.

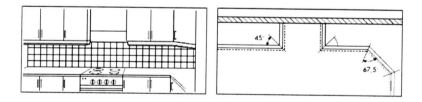

First mark the molding with the angles.

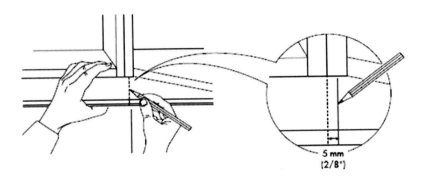

Then cut using the miter saw.

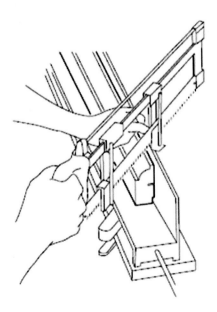

Again use the brackets to mount them on the cabinets.

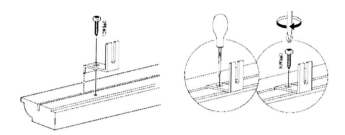

Attach them to the front of the cabinets using the brackets and screws.

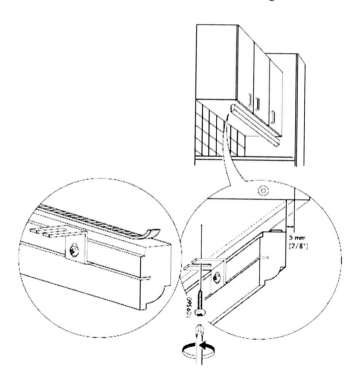

For more polish use crown moldings at the tops of the cabinets.

Use 3M two faced tape to attach them to the top of the cabinets. There is not enough room to get a screw driver in there. You can also use liquid nails to attach them to the tops of the cabinets.

Now attach the Doors and Drawers

Hinges

The hinges are easy to install into the doors. The holes are precut. Just insert the hinges in the precut holes in the doors and pull the level down to lock them in. Screw the other part of the hinge into the cabinet.

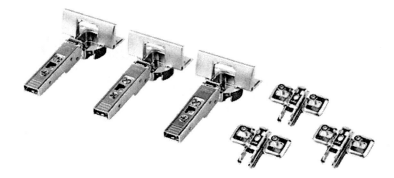

After installed it looks like this.

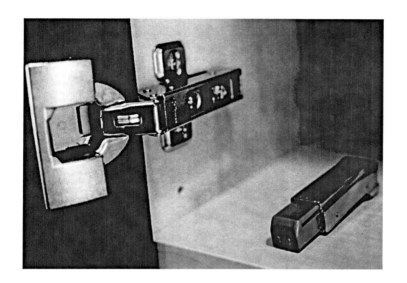

Then install the damper by clicking it on the hinge.

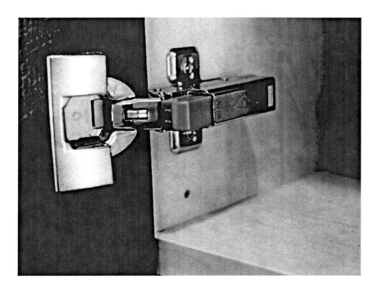

Attaching Door Knobs

First place painting tape over the area you want to drill the door knob hole or holes. You can then use the IKEA drill template to center the holes. Mark the holes with a pen or pencil.

When you drill the holes use a clamp and then place a board on the back of the door and secure it with a clamp. When you drill through the door you will have a good hole coming out the back and not one that is ragged or with split wood.

This is what it looks like after the knobs are installed and tape is removed.

Above the Microwave

If you want to vent your microwave out you'll need to run tubing through the wall outside. The electric plugs for the microwave are also behind the cabinet.

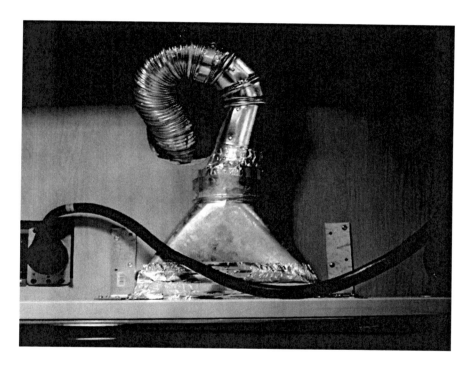

Plumbing Sink and Dishwasher

Generally it is advisable to replace the old valves and pipes in a new kitchen. Leaking valves are the main reason for damage to kitchens.

Building a box under the garbage disposal makes it easy to install it under the sink. This is an invention of mine. Just put the disposal on the box, push it in and lift the disposal up and twist until it locks onto the drain connection.

Planning Granite on the Countertops

It is my opinion that granite is one of the best investments in a house. It is a great selling point. Most people now demand a house with granite countertops.

Measuring the Countertop

When you go out to shop first you need to get a rough idea of the number of square feet you will need. So measure all counter tops and calculate the number of square feet. It is easy just multiply the wide and length in feet of each section and add them all up. The square feet I needed for my kitchen was 55 square feet.

Draw the rough layout of your kitchen counter tops and put the measurements on the paper and take it to HomeDepot, Lowes and some local granite countertop companies and get estimates. Get at least three estimates. Also ask for warranties and guarantees that you would get. I found that Home Depot had the best guarantee – 15 years.

Pick out the color from the samples you like at the show rooms.

Then pick out the edge you want. The standard edge usually is no charge. All of the premium edges cost more. Home Depot many times will run sales on the premium edges. I chose the eased edge, some companies call it double radius. They will also charge you for the number of round corners that you have in the kitchen and if you have an under mount sink installed.

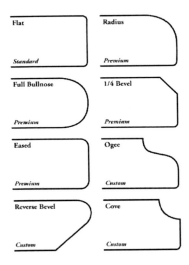

Laser Measurement

Many of the high end granite companies will come out and do a template of your counter top. They use a laser to do this to give them precise measurements.

It actually takes a person up to 2 hours to do a precise laser counter top template. If you should for some reason change the design and want another template, it may cost you an additional $250.

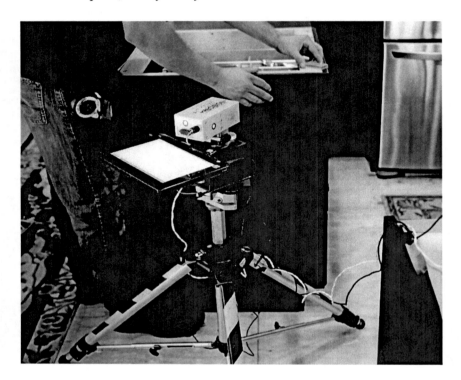

You will be asked to go out to the granite warehouse and pick out the slabs for your counter top. This is the one that I picked out for our kitchen.

They will use high end machines to cut the slabs to the exact template measurements and polish the edges.

You can see the final cut and polished counter tops on carts ready to go out to the customer.

Countertop Brackets and Corbels

If you have any overhangs you will need brackets or corbels.

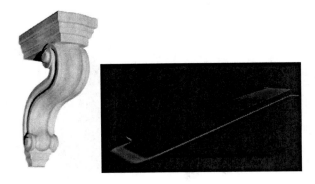

For the IKEA cabinets I recommend that you use special brackets designed especially for IKEA European style cabinets rather than using corbels. They are out of the way and you don't hit your knees on them.

These brackets are available at www.countertopbracket.com

They are installed by using a router in the front of the counter and two screws on the back. See pictures below.

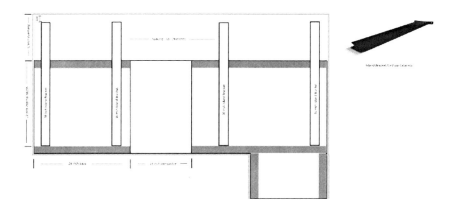

The brackets look nice and are out of the way of your knees.

Granite Installation

Before the installers can put granite on your kitchen cabinets it is necessary for you to remove any and all items out of the base and wall cabinets. Also prepare for dust control as sometimes they will use a grinder or drill during the installation. Make sure your brackets are installed.

Level the Stove

After your countertop in installed you need to raise up and level your stove.

Use a crow bar and adjust all 4 levers on the bottom of the stove so that the counter top matches the sides of the counter top.

Under-Cabinet Lighting

Perhaps the best under counter lighting to use in your IKEA kitchen is the new flexible strip lighting manufactured by www.InspiredLED.com. It gives you the ability to completely design your lighting and install it easily and quickly. It uses newly developed solder less Tiger Paw LED Connectors. These allow you to create custom length LED flex strips. Anyone can do it and putting them on IKEA cabinets is quick and easy. It is not even necessary to drill a hole using IKEA cabinets. The strips have adhesive backs and you can just stick on to the underside of the cabinets.

The LED light strips go behind the moldings at the bottom of the upper cabinets. Cut them to the width of the cabinets. Then attach them to the Tiger Paw LED Connectors. Then run the interconnect cables between the connectors. Connect the end to a switch and then to the 12 volt plug-in power supply.

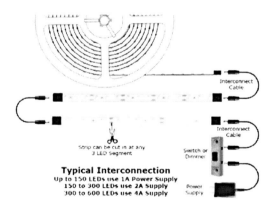

What makes it work so nicely on IKEA cabinets is that there is approximately ¼" space behind the IKEA kitchen cabinets. So you can just pull out the cabinets and stick the wires behind the cabinets. Not necessary to drill holes into the cabinets.

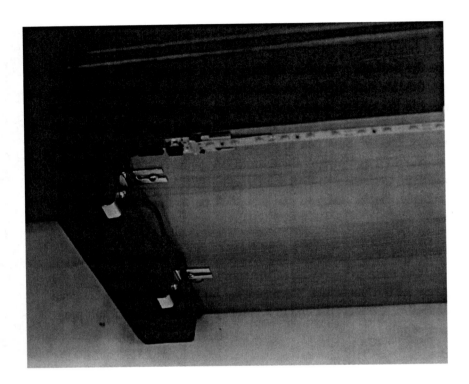

This is a video on how to use this lighting.

http://www.youtube.com/watch?feature=player_embedded&v=Gei_z3-AEwg

If you need help in designing your configuration of lighting you can always call www.inspiredled.com at 480-941-4286. They will help you and give a design via email which is a top notch service. This is the design they gave me:

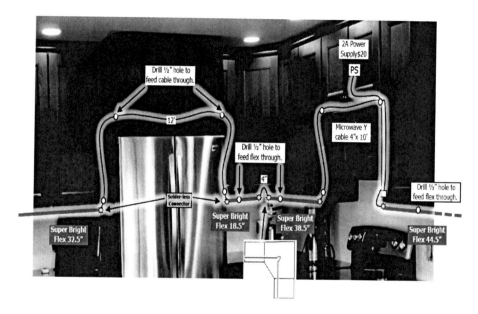

They recommended that I use the Super Bright Flexible Strip 12 Meter Kit below:

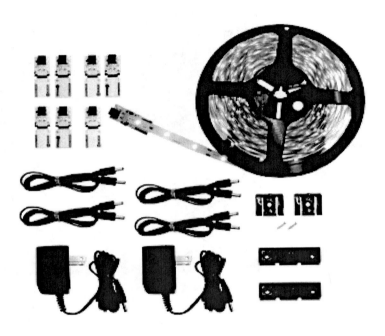

This is how the kitchen looks after the installation of the LED lights:

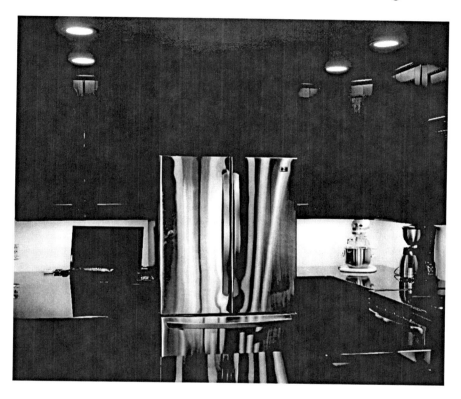

BackSplash

The backsplash is the final part of your IKEA kitchen makeover. With this you can exercise your mindset and express yourself with an inspired backsplash. The key is to have a complete plan with all of the backsplash materials on hand before you start.

IKEA offers usually only two backsplashes which are black and white. These are neutral colors as seen below.

If you want more of a selection I would recommend going to Lowes, Home Depot or your local tile store and see what they had that would interest you for your particular kitchen. At Home Depot and at Lowes you can buy the samples that you like and bring them back for a full refund later on of what you don't want. Take the samples and put them up on your backsplash area and see what matches your cabinets, countertop, and wall color. Also compare prices to get the best deal.

First you need to know how much tile you will need on this project. Use a tape measure to determine both the length and height and then it is good to add 10 percent to it to allow for any waste.

Then go back to the store and buy the amount of the tile that you need for your project.

For this project you will need:

1) Tile
2) Trim if needed
3) Tile Adhesive
4) Un-sanded Grout
5) Stone Sealer
6) Tile Spacers 3/32", 1/16" or 1/8".
7) Orbital sander
8) V-Notched trowel
9) Tape Measure
10) Wet Tile saw
11) Dusk mask and eye protection
12) Vacuum Cleaner
13) Grouting sponge
14) pencil
15) Painters Tape
16) Level

This the wet tile saw I used. It was the Skilsaw below.

First use a level to make sure the countertop is level. Mark the edges with pencil so you know where the tiles end.

You might want to use a product called SimpleMat instead of mortar. It replaces mortar. The adhesive retains its bonding strength for extended periods of time so you have time to position the tiles. You can then grout immediately.

First stick on the SimpleMat and press it to the wall. Get out any bubbles by pressing it firmly to the wall.

Now apply full tiles where the backsplash meets the countertop. Start on the bottom and move up. The tiles on the boarder and directly under the cabinet will need to be cut. As you apply tile insert spacers under the tile to create the gaps that will later need to be filled with grout. Under the bottom line of tiles it will need to later be filled with caulk.

Turn off the electric power and loosen the screws holding the outlets in the electrical boxes. Now pull the outlets out so the tile can fit under the clips. This will bring the boxes flush with the surrounding tile so you don't need box extenders.

For the tiles you need to cut use a pencil or pen to mark the tiles. Use a square to measure and mark the tile. Use the wet tile saw to cut the tiles. Don't force the tile through the cutter too fast. You want the cut to be smooth. Position the tiles around the outlets by sliding them under the metal clips.

As you go make sure everything is level using a spirit level.

Press the tiles firmly again on the SimpleMat. Put the spacers in to get your spacing as you go.

Now mix your grout following the manufacturer's instructions. Stir the grout in a container. Mix only what you need. Allow it to stand for 10 minutes before you use it

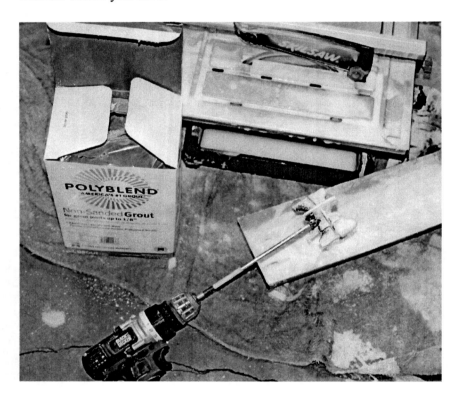

Now apply the grout in small areas, clean it once it begins to haze over. Check for any gaps in the grout. Once the grout cures in 24 to 48 hours then seal the tile using sealer an a soft cotton cloth. Then apply the grout to the spaces between the tiles. Let it set for 5 – 10 minutes. Wipe clean with a sponge.

Now let it set for 24 hours. Then clean off any remaining grout.

Now seal the grout with a good sealer and a sponge.

Finally, caulk between the countertop and backsplash. Wet your fingertip to smooth the caulk line and wiping off any with a paper towel.

You may need to recut your molding to fit the new tile with a jigsaw.

Then it will fit the tile as seen in the picture below.

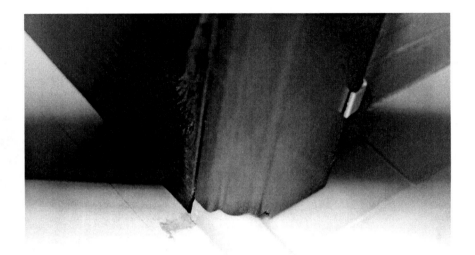

To make the kitchen as modern as possible, you might want to replace the old sockets with new ones.

Pull out the old sockets. Cut and strip the wire. Then attach the wires to the new sockets. Since the sockets need to be extended to the tile you may need to use spacers.

Be careful and turn off the power on the circuit you are working on. Check it with to be sure before you touch any electrical wire with the VoltAlert.

New sockets and plates make the kitchen more modern.

KITCHEN COOKING SOFTWARE

After you get your new kitchen you need to incorporate good cooking software. One of the best software packages is called Cook'n. It might be the only cookbook you'll ever need.

The reasons most families don't have a good diet are the following:

1) First, they don't have an efficient kitchen to cook in. Their stove is not good. The sink does not work for cleaning pots and pans and the dishwasher does a poor job. Basically they don't have a good kitchen to produce the meals they need for good nutrition.

2) Second is that they have little or no planned menus. Usually both the husband and wife work and when they get home at the end of

the day there is no plan for dinner and they either pick up something like fast food or cook something quick and easy, both of which are usually unhealthy food.

3) Third they don't have an organized method to shop and to get the right ingredients they need to cook with.

4) Fourth, they don't have the recipes to cook with and don't really know how to follow them or even how to cook high quality, good tasting, healthy meals.

Because many families pickup fast food at drive thru restaurants like McDonalds, Kentucky Fried Chicken, etc. the food they get is mostly fried, and is most of the time both unhealthily and fattening. This is the reason the country is in a health crisis and 60% are overweight.

I do highly recommend that you incorporate Cook'n Software into your new kitchen. It will solve all of the problems above if you learn how to use it and incorporate it into the new kitchen and your lifestyle.

It allows you to make custom menus and meal plans. You can create the menus for the days, weeks and even months ahead. The software even creates a complete shopping list from the recipes that you add to menu planner. It even categorizes the list making shopping much easier.

The ability to drag and drop recipes into your meal plan makes this software easy to use.

Cook'n software has a lot of support options such as a large list of FAQs on their site. They have excellent support via email. You can also use their user forum and blog. They also have excellent video tutorials on their website.

So with this software you know what to make for the week or even weeks ahead and you have all of the ingredients you need to make the dinners because it is very easy to shop with a categorized list. No more last minute scrambling to go out to get the ingredients. No more running out to get fast food for dinners because you can think of anything to make.

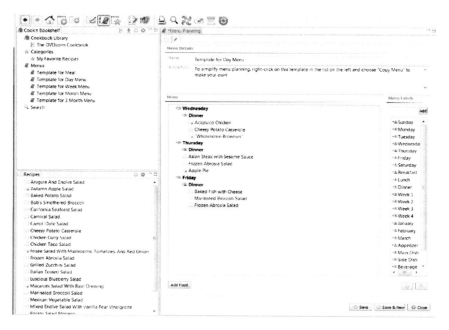

With your new kitchen and Cook'n software you can make healthy lifestyle changing meals and improve your family's health. When you print out a recipe Cook'n gives you the ability to include nutritional information under the recipe. So you can actually plan menus based on the dietary needs of the family.

Cook'n software has a nice function that allows you to print out your menu plan so you can post it on the fridge. Everyone in the family knows what is for dinner every day of the week. No more asking "what's for dinner".

Cook'n will import Pinterest recipes into the software. You can also scan recipes into the program. This will allow you to get recipes that are clipped from magazines and newspapers. You can capture internet recipes with just a click of the mouse button.

Instead of browsing the various sites such as allrecipes.com, foodnetwork.com and other sites for recipes just use Cook'n. As soon as any new recipe is posted on the web it will appear in Cook'n. You can customize you recipe feed and even follow your favorite websites. When you see a recipe you like on these sites just click the recipe and save it to your Cook'n software.

So consider this Cook'n software also as an addition to your new IKEA kitchen.

For more information go to: www.dvo.com

BONUS – TOP SECRET TIPS TO SAVE BIG MONEY

Thank you for purchasing this book. I believe that it will help you create the kitchen of your dreams and save you thousands of dollars.

There are a few top secret tips that could save you additional money that you should know.

If you do me a favor and go to www.Amazon.com and do a review of this book and rate it 4-5 stars, I will email you these secrets.

After you do the review, just email me with a link to the review at tradersworld@gmail.com and I will email back those secrets.

COPYRIGHT

DISCLAIMER

This is an independent book and is not authorized by Inter IKEA Systems B.V. All images of IKEA products, the IKEA Home Planner or any other materials are copyright of Inter IKEA systems B.V. All of the information contained in this book is offered as an accumulation of my experience from planning, designing and installing my IKEA cabinets.

This book has evolved out of my desire to help anyone who is looking to remodel their kitchen on a budget using IKEA cabinets.

It is not my intention to otherwise impersonate any IKEA store or their services. I do not sell IKEA products. Those products are sold solely in the IKEA Retail System – which is franchised by Inter IKEA Systems B.V. of the Netherlands. I am not affiliated in any way with IKEA or their workers, affiliates, partners, sales representatives nor am I financially sponsored by Inter IKEA Systems B.V.

By reading this book you hereby release and discharge the publisher, author and participants from any and all liability, claims, demands or causes of action that you now have now, or may have in the future for injuries, damages, death and or loss of any kind of natural arising in whole or in part from any and all activities, advice or information contained herein in this book. You further agree that if you or someone under your supervision used the information in this book you assume all risks of injury, damage and economic loss, without limitation, and release providers from all liability.

The publisher and author of this book assume no responsibility for the content of any links in this book to third parties.

CPSIA information can be obtained at www.ICGtesting.com
Printed in the USA
BVOW03s0209111213

338794BV00008B/84/P